Emma Pike Ewing

A Text-Book of cookery : for use in Schools

containing an Undergraduate course of Study

Emma Pike Ewing

A Text-Book of cookery : for use in Schools
containing an Undergraduate course of Study

ISBN/EAN: 9783744789578

Printed in Europe, USA, Canada, Australia, Japan

Cover: Foto ©Paul-Georg Meister /pixelio.de

More available books at **www.hansebooks.com**

Household Economics Series

A TEXT-BOOK OF COOKERY

FOR USE IN SCHOOLS

CONTAINING AN UNDERGRADUATE COURSE OF STUDY

BY

EMMA P. EWING

Author of " The Art of Cookery."

"Whatever you wish to introduce into the life of a nation, you must introduce into the schools."—*Froebel.*

MEADVILLE PENNA
FLOOD AND VINCENT
The Chautauqua-Century Press
1897

Copyright, 1897,
By FLOOD & VINCENT

The Chautauqua-Century Press, *Meadville, Pa.*, *U. S. A.*
Electrotyped, Printed, and Bound by Flood & Vincent.

PREFACE.

HOUSEHOLD ECONOMICS—the science of the relation between efforts and satisfactions of a household—includes the science of the relation between efforts and satisfactions in the culinary department of that household. Consequently, cookery becomes a very important branch of household economics and should have as thorough study as any other branch of that science.

The health and well-being of the different members of every family depend largely upon wholesome food, properly prepared, and the head of every family should have a knowledge of the physical needs of each member thereof, and understand how to meet them. It is not necessary for her to know how to prepare complicated dishes and costly compounds; but it is necessary for her to know what food principles the crude materials contain, and how and in what proportion they should be grouped in a meal; and also in what articles the material needed is to be had at the least cost. But, above all, it is important for her to know how this food should be cooked so as to develop and preserve its nutritive qualities, and to render it most appetizing and digestible.

A thorough knowledge of how to select, prepare, and cook the daily rations of the people would vastly improve the physical condition of the race, and greatly aid in the solution of some of the problems that to-day are causing a widespread feeling of anxiety among all classes of earnest men and women.

CONTENTS.

PART I.—FOOD: ITS PROPERTIES AND PREPARATION.

Chapter.		Page.
I.	Food	9
II.	Why We Cook Food	12
III.	Methods of Cooking	14
IV.	Methods of Instruction	19
V.	Suggestions to Teachers	22

PART II.—AN UNDERGRADUATE COURSE IN COOKERY.

First Term.

Lesson.		Page.
I.	Cooking	29
II.	Broiling	30
III.	Baking and Roasting	32
IV.	Boiling	35
V.	Boiling	38
VI.	Frying and Sautéing	42
VII.	Mixing	44
VIII.	Mixing	59
IX.	Mixing	60
X.	Mixing and Seasoning	64
XI.	Salads	66
XII.	A Luncheon	68

Second Term.

I.	Broiling	69
II.	Roasting and Stewing	73

Lesson.		Page.
III.	Boiling	76
IV.	Steaming and Stewing	78
V.	Frying	80
VI.	Mixing	82
VII.	Mixing	85
VIII.	Mixing	87
IX.	Mixing	90
X.	Mixing and Seasoning	91
XI.	Mixing	94
XII.	A Breakfast	97

Third Term.

I.	Broiling, Baking, and Mixing	98
II.	Baking	100
III.	Boiling	103
IV.	Boiling and Mixing	105
V.	Mixing and Frying	108
VI.	Mixing	110
VII.	Mixing	112
VIII.	Mixing	114
IX.	Mixing	117
X.	Mixing	119
XI.	Ice Cream and Ices	121
XII.	A Dinner	122

APPENDIX.

I.	Individual Proportions	125
II.	Utensils Required for Twelve Pupils in a Classroom	127
III.	Reference Books for Teachers	129

PART I.

FOOD: ITS PROPERTIES AND PREPARATION.

A TEXT-BOOK OF COOKERY.

PART I.—FOOD: ITS PROPERTIES AND PREPARATION.

CHAPTER I.

FOOD.

"FOOD," says Professor Atwater, "is that which, taken into the body, builds tissue or yields energy. The most healthful food is that which is best fitted to the wants of the user. The cheapest food is that which furnishes the largest amount of nutriment at the least cost. The best food is that which is cheapest and most healthful."

Professor Voit, of Munich, Germany, estimates that for the maintenance of bodily health a man at hard work requires daily 4 ounces of protein, 4 ounces of fats, and 18 ounces of carbohydrates. Taking into account the more active life in the United States, Professor Atwater suggests that, under similar conditions, a man needs 5 ounces of protein, 5 ounces of fats, and 18 ounces of carbohydrates. A man at moderate labor is supposed to require one ounce less of protein, one ounce less of fats, and two ounces less of carbohydrates. It is estimated that women require still less food, about 3¾ ounces of protein, 2¼ ounces of fats, and 14⅔ ounces of carbohydrates. Children from seven to fifteen years of age require about 3 ounces of protein, 1⁶⁄₇ ounces of fats, and 10⅝ ounces of carbohydrates.

Protein is the chief nutritive element of meat, fish, and eggs. The albumen of eggs, the casein of milk, and the gluten of wheat are protein compounds. These compounds are found in corn, beans, potatoes, and other vegetable food. They are sometimes called nitrogenous compounds, because they contain the element nitrogen, which is not found in the other classes of food. The gelatinoids are the principal ingredients of meat tendon and similar tissues. The albuminoids are the chief ingredients of muscle. Another class of nitrogenous substances in meat are called extractives. The term protein includes albuminoids, gelatinoids, and extractives. The term proteids is sometimes used in place of protein.

Fat is that which we get from meat in the form of tallow and lard, from milk in the form of butter. From vegetables we get olive oil, cottonseed oil, etc. Wheat and corn also contain oil. In fact, fat is found to some extent in most food materials.

Starch and sugar are called carbohydrates. They are very similar in chemical composition. Starch in large proportion is found in rice, potatoes, wheat, and corn. Sugar abounds in many vegetables, as well as in fruits.

Mineral matter is a constituent of meats and fish. It

is also found in smaller proportions in vegetables and fruits. When food materials containing it are burned it remains in the form of ash.

Water is a large and necessary constituent of food material, varying indefinitely in quantity. But the water in food material has no nutritive value beyond any other water.

These nutrients are used in the body in the following ways: Protein forms tissues (muscle, tendon, etc., and fat) and serves as fuel. Carbohydrates are converted into fat and serve as fuel. The fats are used in building up the fatty tissues. They also serve as a concentrated form of fuel. And all yield energy in form of heat and muscular strength. Mineral matter is an essential ingredient of the bones.

QUESTIONS ON CHAPTER I.

1. What is food?
2. Name the principal constituents of food material.
3. In what foods is protein most abundant?
4. Into what three classes are the protein compounds divided?
5. What are the two substances classed as carbohydrates?
6. What are the sources of fat?
7. In what foods are mineral substances found?
8. How is protein used in the body?
9. How are the carbohydrates used?
10. How are the fats used?

CHAPTER II.

WHY WE COOK FOOD.

COOKING produces various chemical and physical changes in food material. It renders the albumen of meat more or less firm, softens the connective gelatinous tissues, and makes the meat more easy of mastication and digestion. The starch in all vegetable food material exists in the form of granules. These are softened by heat and moisture, and thus are made ready to be acted upon by the digestive fluids. Starches are also sometimes changed, by cooking at a high temperature, into dextrin, and sugar is similarly changed into caramel, which are more digestible forms of these foods.

In the cooking of fats there is a softening of the cellular tissue and a slight separation of the glycerine from the fatty acids, thereby rendering them more easily available.

We also cook food to give it warmth. Warmth increases the stimulating effect of food, and causes an increased supply of blood to the digestive apparatus and a greater secretion of digestive fluids.

Cooking also destroys parasites and dangerous bacteria, when the heat is sufficiently intense.

But perhaps the most important of all changes in food material brought about by cooking is the development of flavor. Several eminent authorities hold the opinion that no food is ever perfectly digested and assimilated by the human system unless it be relished in the eating.

Estimates for feeding people are based upon the amount of nutrients contained in the food material before it is cooked. In what degree cookery enhances or diminishes this food value is a problem so subtle and complex that few of even our best chemists have attempted to grapple with it. Yet all admit that the processes of cookery may destroy and eliminate the food value contained in the material in its uncooked state; and that bad cookery may convert wholesome, nutritious food into a poisonous substance, and thus render it an agent of physical destruction instead of a power for recuperation. It is obvious, therefore, that it is of comparatively small importance to know what food the body requires, and the exact amount of each food principle contained in different materials, unless one knows how to prepare and cook those materials in such manner that they can be digested and assimilated by the user.

QUESTIONS ON CHAPTER II.

1. How does heat affect albumen?
2. What effect do heat and moisture have upon starch?
3. Name four reasons for cooking food.

CHAPTER III.

METHODS OF COOKING.

A METHOD of cooking is the particular manner of applying heat to food material to produce certain physical and chemical changes therein, and to render it palatable, digestible, and nutritious.

There are four primary methods of cooking : broiling, baking, boiling, frying. All other methods are merely nominal, being modifications, variations, or combinations of these four primary methods. The action going on within the article being cooked is very similar in character, whether it is being broiled, baked, boiled, or fried. But the flavor and digestibility, as well as the nutritive value of various articles of food, are very differently affected by the different methods of cooking. Every process of cooking can be classified under one or more of these four methods. The process by which the method is applied may be varied ; but the scientific principles which underlie the method must be observed.

Broiling is the sudden searing and browning of the surface of food material. It may be done over a bed of hot coals, before a blazing fire, or above, below, or between blazing gas-jets. The surface of food material may also be seared by bringing it in contact with a heated surface of metal, like a griddle, or, under favorable conditions, by heated air confined in an oven. These are distinct processes of broiling, and all are correct applications of the method if the principle of sudden searing and browning be observed.

Baking is the cooking of food by dry heat: (1) by the application of heated air confined in a close compartment, as in an oven; (2) by bringing the food material in contact with a heated surface, as on a griddle; (3) by roasting before a fire, as in toasting; (4) by burying the food material in hot embers, or with heated stones; (5) by placing the food material in a covered baking dish and surrounding the dish with steam or hot water.

Baking and roasting are terms used interchangeably. The ancient method of roasting before an open fire is seldom practiced at the present time.

Water is said to boil when it reaches a temperature of 212°; and boiling is the cooking of food material in water and certain other liquids when, by the application of heat, these liquids reach the degree of temperature designated the boiling point. Steaming and stewing are modifications of boiling.

Frying is the cooking of food material in oil or fat at a high temperature. The temperature of the oil or fat in which food is to be fried should be as high as the material to be fried will bear.

Sautéing is a modified or less perfect process of frying in which only enough fat is used to prevent the food material from adhering to the griddle or pan, while browning.

In all these methods of cooking the exact degree of heat should be that best adapted to the perfect cooking of the most prominent food principle in the material to be cooked.

In addition to the four primary methods of cooking there are two important subjects connected therewith which should be studied as such: mixing and seasoning. All culinary operations in the preparation and cooking of food can be classified under one or more of these six subjects: broiling, baking, boiling, frying, mixing, and seasoning.

Mixing is the manner of manipulating and combining materials in the process of preparing food. Mixing, as a culinary subject, covers a broad field of work. It includes all manner of manipulations, from the delicate turning over and over of the fragile lettuce leaves in the salad bowl to the severe pounding of the beaten biscuit; from the gentle folding of the feathery omelet soufflé to the strong, brisk beating of batters and the vigorous kneading of bread. Mixing also includes the mingling of few or many, similar or diverse, ingredients in one mixture, as well as the various manipulations necessary under widely different conditions. Mixing necessarily infringes on the subject of seasoning, as the mingling together or mixing of differently flavored food materials is one important form of seasoning.

The object of seasoning food is to develop, modify, or change its flavor, thus rendering it more palatable and nutritious. And with this object in view, salt, sugar, herbs, spices, extracts, condiments, etc., are added to the food in such kind and proportion as are necessary to produce the desired result. If it be true that relish for food is a prominent factor in its perfect digestion and assimilation, seasoning becomes a subject of paramount importance. Proper seasoning stimulates the natural flavor of the food material when weak and insufficient, tones it down when too pronounced and obtrusive, and modifies and changes it when the flavor is not desirable. We season food, therefore, for three reasons: (1) to bring out and develop the natural flavor; (2) to tone down, soften, and render less apparent the natural flavor; (3) to disguise, change, and overcome the natural flavor.

Salt is almost universally used in seasoning food. It seems to possess great power to bring out or develop flavor. That amount which brings out the finest flavor of a food is the proper amount to use; and careful observation proves that the more delicate the flavor of the food the less salt is required. Some edibles are improved in flavor by having salt cooked with them, others by being salted when eaten.

Sugar ranks next to salt in importance for seasoning food. It may be legitimately used in cooking food material that is of a poor quality, when such material, at its best, contains a greater percentage of sugar. Sweet corn, green peas, onions, and beets are prominent examples. The sugar should be added when the material is put to cook. A small quantity of sugar may be used with salt in the seasoning of fresh pork and veal. One third as much sugar as salt sifted together and sprinkled upon either veal or pork just before cooking enriches the flavor. Many fruits are over-sweetened. Too much sugar destroys the fine flavor of the fruit. In sweetening most cooked fruits the sugar should be added just before removing from the fire.

The use of decided flavors, such as spices and pungent herbs, should be generally avoided in the first cooking of meats, poultry, vegetables, and all food material, when the natural flavor is delicate and desirable. Most foods are richest in flavor when freshly cooked. Cold meats are appropriately served with pungent or spicy sauces, and reheated meats may be stimulated in flavor by condiments or sweet herbs.

The fact should never be lost sight of that we season food to render it more palatable, digestible, and nutritious ; not to give the taste of the seasoning to the food, but to render finer and more potent the flavors of the edible seasoned.

Food preparations, such as cakes, creams, and whips, should be carefully flavored, as the fine flavor they should possess is the chief reason for their being.

QUESTIONS ON CHAPTER III.

1. What are the four primary methods of cooking ?
2. Why is broiling put first ?
3. What is the underlying principle of broiling ?
4. How many distinct processes of broiling are there ?
5. In how many ways may heat be applied in baking ?
6. What is boiling ?
7. How does the method of frying differ from that of boiling ?

CHAPTER IV.

METHODS OF INSTRUCTION.

For various reasons the six culinary subjects should be arranged for study in the order here given: (1) broiling; (2) baking; (3) boiling; (4) frying; (5) mixing; (6) seasoning.

According to the best ethnological students, broiling was the first method of cooking practiced by our earliest ancestors. There is little doubt that this was the first method, because it is the simplest process of cooking food, and can be perfectly performed without habitation or cooking utensils of any sort, fire being the one necessary adjunct. These same delvers into antiquity assert that baking and roasting were the methods next put into practice, which was done by placing the food before the fire, or by burying it in hot embers. No food was cooked by boiling until human ingenuity had constructed a rude vessel to hold water, the heating of which was effected by the addition of hot stones.

Frying is a comparatively modern method, and in its simplest operations is only the substitution of oil or fat for water or other liquid.

The arrangement of culinary subjects in the order given in the accompanying "Undergraduate Course in Cookery" (Part II.) is the result of much thought, research, and experimental work in teaching cookery. The writer is convinced that it is a serious error to begin instruction in cooking with complex methods where many problems are involved, as in boiling, rather than with a simpler method (broiling), where the student has only to consider the effect of dry heat upon the food material to be cooked.

Not only is broiling the simplest method of cooking with which we have to deal, but it is the first step in the second method, that of roasting or baking, and naturally leads to its consideration.

Having well considered and thoroughly comprehended the scientific principles involved in broiling and baking, one is better prepared to grapple successfully with those of boiling, in which questions of a more complex nature arise, such as the constituents of water, the different effects of these upon food materials of various kinds, the effect of climate in determining at what temperature water boils, etc. Having mastered all these questions by discovering the scientific solution, the student will readily understand why fat or oil can be made hotter than water, and why for that reason frying may be one of the best and most hygienic methods of cooking food.

The study of frying as naturally follows that of boiling as roasting that of broiling. And as frying is a very convenient and appetizing method of preparing many articles of food it should receive careful consideration.

Mixing is a very complex subject, and it is not easy to determine just where to begin its classification and study. However, it seems best to begin with the simplest manipulations and mixtures, and gradually advance to the mixing which becomes mingling and compounding, and naturally introduces seasoning, a distinct and most important culinary subject.

CHAPTER V.

SUGGESTIONS TO TEACHERS.

IN the arrangement of the course of study herein presented great care has been taken that the pupil should be led, step by step, from the simplest methods and processes to those more involved and complex. It is recommended that when a method of cooking is first presented, the teacher shall make plain the principles involved in that particular method. Where any food material is brought before the class for the first time, reference should be made to the food chart, and the pupils be clearly shown its important food constituents. The prepared analyses of food material will give a still better idea of food constituents than the food chart and should be used frequently. In those the actual food material, separated into its various constituents and in its exact proportions, is before the pupil. It is something very tangible, and makes a deeper impression than mere drawings.

It is highly important that the pupils learn the effect of heat, or of heat and moisture, upon different food constituents, and how the different methods of cooking, when applied to these constituents, prepare them for the various processes of digestion.

In the second lesson a fine opportunity is given for such instruction, in the broiling of beef and the toasting of bread. And an equally favorable one occurs in the third lesson of the first term, in the roasting of beef and the cooking of potatoes in various ways.

At the first presentation of a new subject, whether it be a method of cooking or a manipulation of food material, it is recommended that the teacher demonstrate every step of the process, so the pupil may see the work performed in the best manner before attempting to do it. Even so simple a process as paring an apple or a potato should be properly taught.

It is also recommended that but a single subject be under consideration at one time, and that every pupil in the classroom give close attention to that one subject. Individual practice should be given, but it should be that of most practical value. Very small divisions may be best for children and industrial-school work, where material is of more value than time and where the pupil needs practice in simple addition and subtraction. But for grown-up, well-educated people to divide an egg into half a dozen portions before cooking seems questionable economy.

The group method of practice is recommended when a class is large. But not more than four pupils should work in a group, and group No. 1 should follow the demonstration given by the teacher—each member of the group doing all the work, and completing the article or dish while the teacher and the other pupils observe the process. Then group No. 2 might go through the same formula, if a difficult one, while the first and third groups observe. A slight change or variation might be introduced into the second and third group practice, if the formula were simple.

The three puddings in Lesson X., first term, are an illustration of this suggestion. Great confusion arises when different members of a class are permitted to prepare different dishes at the same time. Each pupil tries to see what is being done in the way of preparing some other dish than the one she herself is working upon. Consequently she obtains only an imperfect knowledge of the dish she is preparing, and a still more imperfect knowledge of that which her neighbor prepares. "One thing at a time, and that done well," is as applicable to the cooking as to the kindergarten class.

When pupils become familiar with the scientific principles which underlie simple methods of cooking and have learned to apply them in the simpler processes of broiling, baking, boiling, and frying, the teacher may, at her discretion, and in harmony with the accompanying course, group different subjects in one lesson; or even permit the pupils to do original work by combining two or three simple preparations into one more complex and elaborate, at the same time requiring the pupil to give the scientific reasons for such combinations and mixtures. To make a new dish at the present time is a doubtful benefit, and when a good reason for mixing different food materials cannot be found, it is safest to abstain from mixing them, lest the result be an incongruous mess.

The time allowed for each lesson is two hours. This

does not include time consumed in washing dishes or taking notes, and it is recommended that the pupils be not required to take notes, but that printed formulas be given them at the close of the lesson. For convenience in giving the lesson the formulas should be upon the blackboard or on a large cardboard, hung so that every pupil can see it easily. Only one formula should be visible at a time. If the teacher gives more than one lesson a day, she should have an assistant to prepare things, so that as far as practicable the work performed by the pupils shall be instructive labor in the strictest sense. Should it be found difficult to give the whole lesson within the two hours, final formulas can be omitted, as the most important instruction comes earliest in the lesson. The lessons are so arranged that when the time allotted to the cooking class is only one hour, the first half of the lesson can be given and the remainder constitute the following lesson, in which case this course of study could occupy two years, instead of being given in one year. Such lessons as cannot be confined to an hour—bread-making and a few others—might be especially arranged for.

To do the best work, the teacher of cookery should be broadly educated and possess a knowledge of all related sciences. But it is well for her to remember that her specialty is the teaching of cookery, and that chemistry, physiology, and hygiene are special studies which enter incidentally into her work, as do also biology, botany, agriculture, geography, physics, etc. All that is positively known in regard to food principles or constituents can be taught incidentally, at the best time for its comprehension, as indicated in the course of study. Incidentally, also, the results of much chemical and physiological research upon the subjects of economic and hygienic living can be brought before the class.

By frequent reference to meat charts—diagrams of cuts of meats—and the food material handled in the lessons, much valuable instruction can be given in marketing.

The proper use and care of cooking utensils is best taught from day to day by insisting upon their proper use and proper care. To devote one or two lessons to this subject as a whole, before the utensils are brought into use, is of doubtful value.

The use of wooden spoons for stirring all manner of food mixtures is strongly urged. The fact that by their use a nerve-distressing clatter is avoided is, perhaps, the least of the many things to be said in favor of them.

All measures should be level or liquid measure. Such measures secure more exactness and also a saving of time. It takes longer to round carefully a spoon with flour or salt than to measure it level full twice.

PART II.

AN UNDERGRADUATE COURSE IN COOKERY.

PART II.—AN UNDERGRADUATE COURSE IN COOKERY.

FIRST TERM.

LESSON I.—COOKING.

ARRANGEMENT OF LESSON.

1. Explain reasons for cooking food.
2. Give methods of cooking food.
3. Explain sources of heat.[1] Natural and artificial.
4. Give the composition of fuels.[2]
5. Give the forms of matter. Changes of the forms of matter through chemical action by which heat is liberated.
6. Define air. Its composition. Active principle.
7. Define the four simple substances found in foods: carbon, oxygen, hydrogen, and nitrogen.
8. Explain how the heat of the body is maintained.
9. Illustrate with candle the necessity of air for combustion.
10. Explain drafts. Construction of stoves.
11. Give the principles involved in the building of fires. Instruction in the management of fires.
12. Give instruction in measuring. Use of utensils in desk.
13. Give instruction in washing dishes.

[1] Youmans's "Handbook of Household Science," p. 17.
[2] Youmans's "Handbook of Household Science," p. 49.

LESSON II.—BROILING.

Arrangement of Lesson.

1. Give instruction in the method of broiling.[1]
2. Show the food principles contained in beef.[2] The important constituent albumen.
3. Show the effect of heat upon albumen.[3] Illustrate by white of egg.
4. Broil steak by open fire.[4]
5. Broil Salisbury steak on griddle.[5]
6. Have pupils broil Salisbury steak.
7. Broil bread. Show difference in the application of heat to the albumen of beef and the starch of bread.[6]
8. Have pupils toast bread.

Formulas for Lesson II.

To Broil a Steak.—Trim neatly by removing with a sharp knife the outer skin and superfluous fat. Fill the broiler compactly, after greasing it, adjusting the meat to the size of the griddle-hole of the stove. Hold close down to the coals or blaze an instant until the under surface of the meat is seared. Turn and sear the other side in a similar manner. Then, by frequent turnings, allow the inside to cook gradually and the outside to brown nicely without becoming hardened. The intense

---

[1] M. Williams's "Chemistry of Cookery," Chapter V.

[2] "Meats: Composition and Cooking." Bulletin No. 34, United States Department of Agriculture.

[3] M. Williams's "Chemistry of Cookery," Chapter III.

[4] Mrs. Ewing's "The Art of Cookery," p. 36.

[5] Mrs. Ewing's "The Art of Cookery," p. 41.

[6] Mrs. Ewing's "The Art of Cookery," p. 40.

heat applied to the under surface of meat in broiling drives the juices toward the opposite surface, and unless the broiler is turned frequently enough to keep both surfaces well seared the juices will be forced out and the meat rendered dry, tough, and innutritious.

Salisbury Steak.—Chop or grind lean round steak very fine, form into cakes, like sausage, and brown on both sides on a griddle or in a spider. Lift to a warm platter, and season with salt, pepper, and butter.

Toast.—When a slice of bread is placed near a clear fire it gradually browns or toasts. The same method of cooking that is termed broiling when applied to meats is termed toasting when applied to bread. Broiling must therefore be varied somewhat in its application to different articles. The heat applied to a steak when first put to broil cannot be too intense, for the best results are obtained when the surface is seared or cooked instantly. But in toasting or broiling bread this is not the case. The application of heat to the slice of bread in order to toast it properly should be gradual, as the object is not to shut in the moisture which the bread contains but to drive it out and gradually dry and brown the surface of the bread. Bread is toasted to divest it of moisture, as well as to brown and give it a peculiar flavor. Toasting converts the insoluble starch in bread into a soluble substance called dextrin, which after being moistened by the saliva is easily digested. For this reason bread properly toasted agrees better with weak stomachs than any other kind of bread.

To Toast Bread.—Cut the bread in even slices about

half an inch in thickness. Slightly dry them in the oven, or before the fire. Put each slice on a toasting fork, or in a wire broiler, and hold it before or over a clear bright fire of coals, but at a sufficient distance from them to allow it to brown evenly without burning. When the surface of one side becomes a rich golden color, turn and toast the other side in a similar manner. Serve in a toast rack, or on a warm plate. Do not pile the slices on each other, or they will lose their crispness and flavor.

LESSON III.—BAKING AND ROASTING.[1]

Arrangement of Lesson.

1. Explain various ways of applying heat in baking.
2. Review briefly the effect of heat upon albumen.
3. Refer to charts to show the various cuts of meat used in roasting.
4. Prepare and put to roast a two-rib, short cut of beef.[2]
5. Grate a potato and remove the starch. Cook the starch and explain how heat and moisture affect starch granules.[3]
6. Have pupils prepare and bake potatoes.
7. Have pupils prepare and bake apples in the skin.
8. Have pupils pare and bake apples.
9. Make roast beef gravy.
10. Carve and serve small portions of the beef with platter gravy; also with the made gravy.

[1] "The Art of Cookery," pp. 46-48.
[2] "The Art of Cookery," p. 49.
[3] Youmans's "Handbook of Household Science," pp. 213, 279.

Formulas for Lesson III.

To Prepare a Roast of Beef.—Remove the outer skin, and with a moist cloth wipe the surface on the inside of the cut wherever it has been exposed to dust. Do not remove the bones.

To Roast Beef.—Place the clean-cut side of the meat upon a smoking hot pan. Press it close to the pan until seared and slightly brown. Reverse it and let the opposite side become similarly seared and brown, then put it at once into the oven, the heat of which should be the same as for bread (370°), and leave it undisturbed till cooked. If the oven is not too hot the meat will require no basting. But when the meat is taken from the pan one cup of water should be added to the drippings therein for making gravy. When the temperature of the oven is correct and the cooking is going on properly the meat will keep up a gentle sputtering in the pan. If, however, smoke should be discernible in the oven the heat is too intense and should be lessened.

For roasting beef in this manner, after it has been seared, fifteen minutes should be allowed for each inch in thickness of the roast, without regard to its width or weight.

To Prepare Potatoes.—If the potatoes are to be baked or boiled in their skins, wash clean, using a small brush to scrub them with, and remove, with a knife, all specks or blemishes. In paring potatoes use a small, thin-bladed, sharp-pointed knife. Drop the potatoes as soon as pared into cold water, and let them remain there until needed for cooking. This keeps them from exposure to the air, and prevents their becoming discolored.

To Bake Potatoes.—Put the potato in an oven of moderate temperature and subject it to a gradually increasing heat, until the inside is thoroughly cooked and the skin has assumed a light brown color and a firm consistency. When baked potatoes are taken from the oven a gash about an inch in length should be made lengthwise in each potato, and the ends should then be pressed, to widen the gash and permit the steam to escape.

To Bake Apples, No. 1.—Select apples of a uniform size, remove the center of the blossom end and any specks, wash and rinse in clean water, place, stems upward, in an earthen or granite-ware baking dish, pierce in several places with a fork, and put in an oven at the temperature required for bread. When perfectly baked the skins will be brown and the flesh soft and rich in flavor.

To Bake Apples, No. 2.—Pare and core the apples, leaving them whole, rinse in cold water, and place close together in a baking dish, the bottom of which has been well greased with butter and lightly sprinkled with granulated sugar. Sprinkle sugar over the apples and bake in a hot oven until they are a rich brown color. Unless the apples are very tart and juicy they should, when put to bake, be covered for about ten minutes.

Roast Beef Gravy.—Cook together until brown one tablespoonful each of butter and flour, add one cup of water from the roasting pan, after it has been strained and skimmed of grease, and simmer five minutes. Serve with the roast beef.

LESSON IV.—BOILING.[1]

Arrangement of Lesson.

1. Explain boiling of water. Use thermometer.[2]
2. Prepare and put to cook a leg of lamb or mutton.
3. Refer to charts for cuts and constituents of mutton.
4. Boil an egg properly and one improperly.
5. Make soup stock.[3]
6. Give instruction in the preparation and cooking of potatoes, cabbage, turnips, and carrots.
7. Have pupils prepare and cook these vegetables.
8. Show by reference to food chart the different proportions of the food principles in the various articles cooked.
9. Give demonstration in the cooking of rice.
10. Make a broth from the lamb or mutton liquor with rice and parsley.
11. Make drawn butter sauce.
12. Show how a leg of lamb or mutton should be carved.

Formulas for Lesson IV.

To Prepare a Leg of Lamb or Mutton.—The outer skin should be carefully removed from both mutton and

---
[1] "The Art of Cookery," pp. 65-68.
[2] "Chemistry of Cookery," p. 8.
[3] "The Art of Cookery," pp. 100-102.

lamb before they are cooked. This is more important in the preparation of mutton and lamb than in the preparation of other meats, as they are liable to have an unpleasant, woolly flavor when boiled or roasted with the skin unremoved.

To Boil a Leg of Lamb or Mutton.—Put the lamb or mutton in a kettle of boiling water, slightly salted, and cook until tender. When sufficiently done take from the kettle and place on a platter. Serve with drawn butter.

To Boil an Egg.—Pour a pint of boiling water into a small sauce-pan or other vessel, put the egg in it, cover closely, place it where it will keep hot, and let stand for about six minutes. An egg so cooked will be evenly done all through without being hard, semi-raw, or slimy, and will be tender, delicate, and delicious. A pint of water should be allowed for each egg.

To hard-boil an egg put it in a pint of boiling water and let it remain there twenty minutes. This will render the yolk dry and mealy. Or put the egg in cold water, bring to the boiling point, and let the egg remain in it for fifteen minutes.

Soup Stock.—To make soup stock, put into a kettle or digester, in cold water slightly salted, meat of any kind cut in small pieces, or meat and bones well cut and broken, heat the water gradually until it reaches the boiling point, then keep it simmering continuously until the juices of the meat are all extracted. When meat and bones are well cut and broken up, all their valuable properties can, by proper cooking, be extracted in four or five hours. After simmering that length of time the kettle should be taken from the fire, and the stock strained through a colander into an earthen bowl.

To Boil Potatoes.—To boil either pared or unpared potatoes, put them in a liberal allowance of slightly salted boiling water, and keep them cooking gently until tender enough to be pierced easily with a fork. Drain off the water, sprinkle a little salt over the potatoes, cover with a towel or napkin, and set the kettle containing them back on the range where they will dry off and keep warm. A medium-sized potato will boil in twenty-five minutes.

To Boil Cabbage.—Trim, wash, and divide each head of cabbage in quarters or eighths, boil till tender, drain, press out the water, and serve with drawn butter.

To Boil Turnips.—Wash and pare the turnips, boil till tender, drain in a colander, press out the water, mash fine, and season with salt, pepper, and butter.

To Boil Carrots.—Wash, scrape, boil till tender, drain, season with butter, salt, and pepper.

To Wash Rice.—Pick over the quantity of rice needed, put it in a bowl, cover with tepid water, lift in the hands and rub the kernels briskly against each other to remove the starch. Rinse in cold water several times, or until the water ceases to look milky, then drain and put at once to cook.

To Boil Rice.—Put a cup of prepared rice into two quarts of boiling water and let it cook rapidly without stirring for fifteen or twenty minutes, or until it becomes so tender that the grains can be crushed between the fingers into a smooth paste. Then drain in a sieve or colander, return to the vessel in which it was cooked, and set on the back of the range to dry off.

Mutton Broth.—To four cups of mutton stock add one cup of boiled rice and one tablespoonful of minced parsley. Simmer five minutes, season to taste, and serve.

Drawn Butter.—Cook together until well mixed one tablespoonful each of butter and flour, add one cup of water or broth, simmer five minutes, then add another tablespoonful of butter. Season and serve.

LESSON V.—BOILING.

Arrangement of Lesson.

1. Prepare veal for stewing.
2. Cook macaroni.
3. Make beef tea.
4. Give instruction in use of double boilers and in cooking cereals.[1]
5. Have pupils cook rolled wheat, rolled oats, cornmeal mush.
6. Have pupils stew apples.
7. Make three gravies, plain, white, brown.
8. Make tea and coffee.[2]

Formulas for Lesson V.

To Stew Veal.—The ribs, breast, and thin pieces

---

[1] "The Art of Cookery," pp. 74-77.
[2] "The Art of Cookery," pp. 77-78.

containing a good deal of fat are the most desirable portions of veal for stewing. Remove the outer skin from one and one half pounds of veal, cut the meat in pieces suitable for serving, put it in a sauce-pan, add a teaspoonful of salt and hot water enough barely to cover the meat. Cover the sauce-pan closely and let the meat cook slowly for three or four hours, or until tender, then drain the broth from it, remove the grease from the broth, add hot water, if necessary, to make three cups of the broth, and make a plain gravy.

To Boil Macaroni.—Break the macaroni in pieces any length desired, put into well-salted boiling water, cook an hour, or until tender enough to be mashed easily with the fingers, then drain in a colander.

Beef Tea.—For making beef tea a cut from the round is preferable on account of its juiciness, and care should be taken to have it as fresh as possible ; and in preparing it the skin and fat should be all removed and the meat cut in small pieces. It should then be put in a kettle or sauce-pan, barely covered with cold water, slightly salted, heated to the boiling point, and strained through a colander. It is then ready for use.

To Cook Cereals.—Fill the outside boiler about two thirds full of boiling water, set the inside boiler or kettle in it, put the proper quantity of boiling liquid in the inside kettle, add the requisite amount of salt, and sprinkle in the grain or meal, stirring slowly until it swells or thickens enough to keep it from settling on the bottom of the kettle, then cease stirring, cover closely, and let it simmer until thoroughly cooked.

Very few cereals can be cooked properly in less than an hour. Most of them require two or three hours' cooking.

Rolled wheat, barley, or oats.—Three cups of liquid to each cup of grain. Cook an hour.

Cracked wheat, coarse oatmeal, granulated hominy.—Five cups of liquid to each cup of grain. Cook two or three hours.

Corn-meal Mush.—Three cups of boiling water, one cup of corn-meal, half a cup of cold water, one teaspoonful of salt. Moisten the meal with the cold water, and stir the mixture gradually into the boiling water, to which the salt has been added. Cook thirty minutes, stirring occasionally to keep it from sticking to the kettle and burning, then move to the back of the stove, and let simmer gently an hour, or until ready to serve.

If the mush is to be used for frying, moisten the meal with cold milk instead of water—as it will brown easier—and after it has cooked half an hour turn it into a pan or mold that has been wet with cold water, and let cool.

To Stew Apples.—Pare, quarter, core, and wash the apples. Place the prepared quarters in a sauce-pan with a small quantity of hot water, cover closely, and stew rapidly for five minutes. Upon removing the cover, the apples, if done, will be broken and so tender as to fall apart readily. If not done, replace the cover and cook a few minutes longer. Put in a bowl or dish half the quantity of sugar required, pour the cooked apples into the dish, sprinkle the other half of the sugar over them, cover closely, and serve hot or warm.

Plain Gravy.—Cook together one tablespoonful of butter and one of flour till well mixed. Add one cup of the veal broth, simmer two minutes, then add to the gravy one third of the stewed veal. Season to taste with salt and pepper.

White Sauce.—Cook together one tablespoonful each of butter and flour. Add three fourths of a cup of veal broth, simmer two minutes, add one fourth of a cup of cream, and when hot add one third of the cooked veal. Season to taste with salt and pepper.

Brown Sauce.—Brown together in a sauce-pan one teaspoonful each of butter and flour, add one cup of veal broth, simmer two minutes, and add the remaining portion of the veal. Season to taste with salt and pepper.

To Make Coffee.—One tablespoonful of finely ground coffee, two tablespoonfuls of cold water, one teaspoonful of white of egg, one cup of boiling water. Mix coffee, egg, and cold water together. Put in the coffee pot and add the boiling water. Simmer five minutes, add a tablespoonful of cold water, and it is ready to serve.

To Make Green Tea.—One half teaspoonful of tea, one cup of water. Have the pot heated, put in the tea, and pour the freshly boiled water upon it. Stand it in a warm place where it will not boil, for five minutes.

To Make Oolong Tea.—Make the same as green, doubling the quantity of tea.

LESSON VI.—FRYING AND SAUTEING.

Arrangement of Lesson.

1. Explain principles involved in frying.[1]
2. Prepare and cut in pieces a fish for frying.
3. Give instruction in the selection and cleaning of fish.[2] In the food principle contained in fish.[3] In the food value of fish.[4]
4. Prepare potatoes for frying.
5. Fry potatoes and fish.
6. Have pupils fry potatoes and fish.
7. Sauté veal chops.
8. Have pupils sauté veal chops.
9. Have pupils sauté bacon.
10. Have pupils sauté liver.
11. Give instruction in preparing bread crumbs for frying.

Formulas for Lesson VI.

To Fry Potatoes.—Prepare the potatoes in any form desired. Let them soak in cold water until wanted for frying. Heat the grease in the frying kettle. Test its temperature with a slice of potato, and if hot enough lower the frying basket into it. Drain the potatoes in a sieve and shake them in a towel to free them of moisture. Place a few slices at a time in the basket until the bottom is covered. The rapidity with which the potatoes may be dropped into the basket must be

---

[1] "Chemistry of Cookery," pp. 84–97.
[2] "The Art of Cookery," pp. 14, 21.
[3] "Foods: Nutritive Value and Cost," Atwater, Bulletin No. 23, p. 27.
[4] "Foods: Nutritive Value and Cost," p. 27.

determined by the appearance of the fat. If the surface of the grease becomes covered with bubbles, it is an indication that its temperature is too low for perfect frying. Wait until the bubbles disappear before adding more potatoes. This test of temperature will apply to the frying of all articles. As soon as the potatoes are sufficiently cooked lift the basket from the grease, shake it over the kettle to free it and its contents from grease, dust the potatoes with salt and pepper, and pour into a warm dish lined with several folds of cheese-cloth.

To Fry Fish.—Cut fresh fish of any kind in pieces a suitable size for serving, and season with salt and pepper, and fry in hot fat until they are a rich brown color and can be pierced easily with a fork. Then drain on cheese-cloth.

To Saute Veal Chops.—Cut the chops an inch thick from the ribs or loin, remove the outer skin, season with sugar, salt, and pepper, and dredge with flour. Have a spoonful of hot clarified butter in a spider over the fire, lay in the chops, brown the under side, and turn them over in the spider. When brown on both sides, cover the spider closely, shove it to the back of the range, let the chops simmer ten minutes, then lift them to a warm platter. Add a tablespoonful of sweet milk to the gravy in the skillet, stir well, and strain over the chops.

Clarified Butter.—To clarify butter heat it to boiling point, and let it simmer gently until the salt settles and a frothy scum arises, leaving the oily portions transparent. Remove the scum, drain the oil carefully from the salt, and the clarified butter is ready for use. Butter in being clarified should never be allowed to scorch or become brown.

To Saute Breakfast Bacon.—Slice thin, remove the rind and brown edges, lay upon a hot spider over a moderate fire until brown on both sides and crisp.

To Saute Calf's Liver.—Remove the skin from the liver, cut in slices half an inch in thickness, soak in salted cold water half an hour, dry on a towel, dust lightly with pepper and freely with flour, and cook gently in a spider in a little clarified butter, or drippings from salt pork or breakfast bacon, until thoroughly done.

Crumbs for Frying.—To prepare crumbs for frying, take pieces of dry bread, crusts, or crackers, lay upon a molding board, and, with a rolling-pin, crush and roll them into very fine crumbs. Sift before using.

LESSON VII.—MIXING.[1]

Bread and Rolls.

ARRANGEMENT OF LESSON.

1. Give instruction in the food principles contained in wheat ; also in the process of making flour.[2]
2. Instruction concerning yeast and yeast fermentation.[3]
3. Mold light dough into loaves and rolls. (Teacher and pupils.)
4. Mix bread dough.

[1] " The Art of Cookery," pp. 179-181.
[2] " The Art of Cookery," pp. 184-186.
[3] " The Art of Cookery," pp. 186-191.

5. Have pupils mix bread dough, each pupil using a half pint of wetting.
6. Bake the loaves and rolls.

FORMULAS FOR LESSON VII.

Bread-making.—Bread-making is a neglected art. In hotels, restaurants, boarding houses, and private families, bad bread is abundant and good bread seldom found. Everywhere bad bread is the rule, good bread the exception. Yet good bread is one of the most nutritious, satisfying, and inexpensive articles of human food, while bad bread is one of the most innutritious, unsatisfying, and expensive.

The general belief that numerous ingredients and much hard labor are necessary for successful bread-making has no foundation in fact. Bread-making, when the principles are understood, is one of the easiest of culinary processes; and the only ingredients needed for bread of the choicest quality are flour, yeast, milk, water, and salt. Women will use salt rising, dry yeast cakes, potato balls, yeast foam, and innumerable other ferments to lighten their dough, and supplement them with grease, sugar, alum, vinegar, charcoal, and almost every other conceivable thing, and invariably have bad bread. Yet it seems never to occur to them to use only the proper ingredients. Why do people take such infinite pains to make bad bread? Why, in this enlightened age of the world, should any person of ordinary sense want salt rising, dried yeast cakes, potato balls, or any false or putrefactive ferments in bread-making, when compressed yeast or pure home-made yeast is so readily obtainable, and is so superior in all respects for the purpose? Or why should any intelligent person put ought else into dough than flour, yeast, milk, water, and salt, when these ingredients alone produce the very best of bread?

In the good old times of which we are so frequently reminded by pessimistic croakers, wheat with a year's accumulation of dirt clinging to it was emptied from a dirty sack into a dirty hopper, crushed by dirty stones into dirty flour, and then mixed with a dirty ferment into grandmother's bread. Was there not, under such conditions, a basis of truth for the then prevalent belief that it was the allotted task of each member of the family to eat his or her peck of dirt? But those conditions have passed away. Through the agency of an improved method of milling, each grain of wheat is carefully brushed free of dirt and furze before it passes under the polished steel or porcelain rollers to be converted into flour, and by the aid of science pure yeast is made expressly for family use. Should not such an advance in preparing flour and yeast be followed by a similar advance in making bread? The flour and yeast of to-day are far superior to the flour and yeast used by our grandmothers. Why should not the bread made to-day be far superior to the bread made by our grandmothers? The flour and yeast furnished by American men to-day are unequaled anywhere in excellence. Why shouldn't the bread made by American women to-day be the best bread in the world?

Flour.—Under the system of milling that was almost universal until thirty years ago the only fine flour that could be produced was mostly starch and the finest white flour was then deficient in nitrogen and the phosphates. Millers had no facilities for separating and purifying the middlings which contained the hard, nitrogenous parts of the grain, and they were largely used for pig and cattle feed. The new system of milling, known as the roller process, has, however, entirely revolutionized things, and the middlings which contained those parts of the wheat are now purified and milled with care into patent or new process flour. The idea is still entertained by many that the choice, high-priced, patent flours are deficient in nitrogenous matter, and that coarse flour is more nutritious and healthful than fine. The reverse is the fact. The finest flours contain all the best elements of the wheat berry, without any admixture of pulverized wood fiber, bran coating, or germ grease ; and, all things considered, the very finest patent flour holds the leading place both hygienically and economically among cereal foods or grain products.

The highest grade of patent flour is made from middlings cleansed from impurities by "middlings purifiers." The inferior middlings go into other grades in due proportion. And the highest grade contains more gluten in proportion to the quantity of starch than the other grades. But any of the different grades of flour made at a certain mill can be raised or lowered in quality at the option of the miller, by increasing or decreasing the amount of gluten and starch in a given quantity of flour. Where the first patent made from a given quantity of wheat is of the choicest quality, it contains a large percentage of the best constituents of the wheat, and the other grades made from the same wheat must be correspondingly low in those constituents. Of course where only one grade of flour is made at a mill all the constituents of the wheat berry go into the flour; but in a hundred pounds of such flour the quantity of starch is greater in proportion to the quantity of gluten than it is in a hundred pounds of the highest grade patent flour. There is usually considerable difference in the price of first and second grade flour, and frequently a difference of fifty per cent in price between a sack of the highest and a sack of the lowest grade flour. In other words, when the best patent flour made by a certain mill sells for $1.50 a sack, the lowest grade flour made by the same mill sells for 80 cents a sack. As a general rule, however, the highest priced flour is the cheapest, as it contains twice the amount of nutritious material and will, with half the labor, produce more than twice the quantity of good, wholesome bread.

Strength, when applied to flour, means the measure of its power to absorb and retain water; or indicates rather the measure of water that the flour will absorb to produce dough of a certain consistency, without any regard to the delicacy or nutritive qualities of the bread obtained from such dough. And when millers and bakers talk of "a strong flour," they mean that a certain grade of flour will absorb more water, and make more loaves of bread, than another grade will, and that a sack of flour of a special grade will take more wetting into its mixture and yield a greater quantity of bread than a sack of another grade will, the quality of the bread not being taken into account.

Spring wheat has a harder grain than winter wheat and yields a harder and grittier flour, which absorbs more water and is easier to handle successfully than winter wheat flour, in bread-making. But equally good bread can be made from either variety, although more delicate cake and pastry can be made from winter wheat than from spring wheat flour, and what is known in the market as "pastry flour" is simply flour made of winter wheat.

Compressed Yeast.—Yeast is a vegetable germ found upon the skin of grapes, plums, and some other fruits—in fact, the beautiful shade upon the skin of those fruits known as "bloom" is produced by the yeast plants that float in the atmosphere settling upon them. If yeast germs get, or are put, into a substance in which they find material adapted to their development they increase very rapidly, and by their vegetative action during the period of growth cause the substance in which they are growing to bubble or ferment. The manufacturers of yeast multiply these germs indefinitely by inducing fermentation in a sweet infusion of malt, rye, and corn, and millions of the germs rise to the surface of the fermenting liquid, forming a scum resembling the froth of new milk. This scum is removed, run into vats of cold water, and allowed to settle to the bottom. The water is then pumped off, and the yeast pumped into hydraulic presses and reduced by pressure to the consistency desired, when it is made into cakes and put upon the market as "compressed yeast." And from the fact that compressed yeast is the purest yeast that scientific research has yet discovered, and that it is impossible by mechanical skill to crowd a greater number of yeast germs into a given space than are crowded into a cake of compressed yeast, it goes almost without saying that compressed yeast is the best ferment known to the world to-day for bread-making.

It has been demonstrated over and over again that a certain quantity of pure, strong yeast is necessary to produce the best results in bread-making—that it is, in fact, impossible to make the best quality of bread unless the proper quantity of yeast be used ; and housekeepers who, to save two or three cents on each baking, buy liquid yeast at the bake shop, or dry yeast cakes at the corner grocery, always have inferior bread and are losers in nearly every way, in the long run. In yeast fermentation the decomposition of the starch in flour yields the gas that lightens the dough, while in these other fermentations it is the gluten that suffers ; and as starch is the most plentiful and least valuable portion of the flour, economical considerations alone should induce the use of compressed yeast in preference to any other ferments. Pure yeast produces sweet, nutty-flavored, wholesome bread, while diseased and putrefactive ferments produce the coarse, rough crumb, the pale, flinty crust, and the flat, sour loaf that are so disappointing and discouraging to the bread-maker. The alleged costliness of compressed yeast would be a serious objection to its use in many families, if the allegation were correct. But no one whose time is of any value can afford to dabble with dry yeast cakes or any of the other ferments. They generally cost a hundred fold more than compressed yeast by annoying the user, by robbing the flour of nutrition, and by yielding inferior bread. How much is gained in a baking by using one cent's worth of common yeast and losing four cents' worth of nutritive matter from the flour, over using four cents' worth of compressed yeast and retaining all the nutrition in the bread?

The liability of compressed yeast to spoil in a short time by exposure is an objection that is frequently made to its use. But a similar objection can, with equal propriety, be made to the use of fresh fish, fowl, and flesh generally. And as a large proportion of so-called perishable articles of food require greater care for their perfect preservation than compressed yeast, this objection is more imaginary than real. As long as compressed yeast remains firm and has an alcoholic smell it can be depended upon to give better results than dry yeast cakes or liquid yeast; but the fresher it can be had the better it is for bread-making, and in localities where it is readily obtainable housekeepers should always get it as fresh as possible.

Given good flour and good yeast any one should be able to make good bread, for the only other ingredients needed are a little salt and sufficient wetting to mix the flour into a dough of the proper consistency. And the wetting may be either water, or milk, or milk and water—provided always the milk is sweet. Bread mixed with water alone is tougher and sweeter, and will keep moist longer than bread mixed with milk and water, or with milk alone. French bread is mixed with water alone, Vienna bread is mixed with milk and water in equal proportions, and several varieties of bread are mixed with milk alone.

Comparatively good bread can be made with liquid yeast, or even with dry yeast cakes if fresh and sweet; but the best quality of bread can be made only with compressed yeast. And bread can be made so much easier with compressed yeast than with either liquid yeast or dry yeast cakes, that no housekeeper who can get compressed yeast can afford to use any other kind.

Compressed Yeast Bread.—To each pint of lukewarm wetting, composed of equal portions of sweet milk and water, add a teaspoonful of salt and one half-ounce cake of compressed yeast dissolved in about three tablespoonfuls of cold water, then stir in flour with a spoon until a dough is formed sufficiently stiff to be turned from the mixing bowl in a mass. Put this dough on a molding board, and knead well, adding flour until it ceases to stick to the fingers or the molding board, then put it in a well-greased earthen bowl, brush the surface lightly with melted butter or drippings to keep it from crusting over, cover it with a bread towel, set to rise, and let stand for three hours, at a temperature of seventy-five degrees. At the end of that time form into loaves or rolls, put into greased pans, brush the surface with melted butter or drippings, cover as before, and again set to rise for an hour, at the same temperature, then bake.

Dough when light enough to bake should be double the size in bulk it was when set to rise, and should be so aerated all through that when lifted in the pan the sense of weight will be scarcely perceptible.

Bread should be put to bake as soon as it is sufficiently light; and the oven, at the time the dough is put into it, should be at a temperature of 375 degrees—or hot enough to brown nicely a spoonful of flour in two minutes—and it should be kept at almost the same temperature throughout the baking. At that temperature rolls will bake in twenty or twenty-five minutes, and ordinary sized loaves in from forty-five to fifty minutes. A loaf of bread when perfectly baked is a beautiful chestnut brown all over. If either the ends, sides, or bottom have a sickly hue, or are perceptibly lighter in color than the top, the loaf has been imperfectly baked, and should be returned to the oven. A loaf of bread when sufficiently baked will not burn the hand, if lifted from the baking pan and laid on the open palm; and if tapped on the bottom with the finger it will emit a hollow sound. Bread not sufficiently baked deteriorates rapidly and will begin to grow moldy, and frequently ropy, in three or four days, while perfectly baked bread may be kept from mold, and in very good condition, for a week or ten days.

Bread as soon as taken from the oven should be turned from the pans, and placed, uncovered, in such position as will expose the greatest amount of surface to the fresh air, without allowing it to come in contact with anything likely to give it an unpleasant taste or odor. And when cold it should be put in a box or jar to which the air can have access, and be kept in a dry, cool room or closet. To wrap bread in cloths while warm prevents the escape of gas or steam, destroys the crispness of the crust, and robs the bread of much of its fine, nutty flavor.

The quantity of flour necessary to be mixed with a certain quantity of wetting to make dough of the proper consistency for bread cannot be given accurately by weight or measure, without knowing the special brand of flour to be used, as the quantity varies according to the quality. But each quart of wetting will require from three pounds and ten ounces to three pounds and twelve ounces, or from seven to seven and one half pints of the best flour, and the amount of dough mixed from these proportions of wetting and flour will make four medium-sized loaves, or about five pounds, of good bread.

The quantity of yeast used in bread-making is quite important. If an insufficient quantity is used the bread will be devoid of the rich, nutty flavor which is a prominent characteristic of all good bread, and will frequently have a yeasty smell or taste.

Bread is never improved by the addition of grease or sugar. Grease interferes with the perfect action of the yeast, and sugar destroys much of the fine flavor of the flour. The simplest, easiest, and best method of making bread that has yet been discovered is the method given above. The formula is that used by the Vienna bakers, who have for many years had the reputation of being the best bread-makers in the world. And all bread made in that manner is known as Vienna bread.

Liquid Yeast.—Compressed yeast is on sale in most towns and villages, but as it cannot be obtained at all times and in all places every housekeeper should be acquainted with some approved method of making liquid yeast. Here is one that has been thoroughly tested: Steep an eighth of an ounce of pressed, or a small handful of loose, hops in a quart of boiling water for about five minutes. Strain the boiling infusion upon half a pint of flour, stirred to a smooth paste with a little cold water, mix well, let boil a minute, add a tablespoonful of salt, two tablespoonfuls of white sugar, set aside till lukewarm, then stir in two half-ounce cakes of compressed yeast dissolved in two tablespoonfuls of cold water, or a gill of good liquid yeast. Let stand twenty-four hours, stirring occasionally, cover closely, and set in a cool place. Yeast made according to this method will keep sweet two or three weeks, and can be used any time during that period for mixing bread, or for starting a fresh supply of yeast.

Liquid Yeast Bread.—Mash one medium-sized, well-boiled potato in an earthen bowl with half a teacupful of flour, and pour over it, stirring meanwhile, a quart of boiling water. Set the mixture aside until it becomes lukewarm, then pour into it half a teacupful of liquid yeast, stir well, cover closely, and let stand till light. When it is perfectly light and foamy, which will be in about six hours if kept at the proper temperature, mix together equal portions of this ferment and warm sweet milk. Stir in sifted flour until a dough is formed sufficiently stiff to be turned from the mixing bowl to the molding board in a mass, then proceed in every respect as when making bread with compressed yeast. Bread made according to this method goes under the general name of home-made bread, and if all the conditions are carefully complied with it will be of good quality, but not nearly so good as Vienna bread.

Imperial Rolls.—Divide a piece of Vienna bread dough, large enough for an ordinary sized loaf, into a dozen irregular pieces about half an inch in thickness. Take, separately, each of these pieces in the left hand, and slightly stretch with the thumb and forefinger of the right hand one of the irregular points over the left thumb, toward the center of the roll. Repeat this operation, turning the piece of dough as it proceeds, at each turn lifting the thumb and gently pressing it upon the last fold, until all the points have been drawn in, when the roll must be turned face, or smooth side, upward to rise, and when sufficiently risen must be reversed in position, or turned smooth side downward in the pan, and placed in the oven. If the folding is done properly, an imperial roll when baked will be composed of a succession of sheets or layers of delicate, tenacious crumb, surrounded with a thin, crisp, tender crust.

French Rolls No. 1.—Take enough dough for a small loaf of bread, and divide it into four pieces. Roll each piece under the palms of the hands, upon the molding board, into a long roll not much thicker than one's thumb, lay in a suitable roll-pan, let rise till sufficiently light, then bake.

French Rolls No. 2.—Divide a piece of bread dough large enough for a small loaf of bread into twelve pieces. With the finger-tips knead each piece into a ball, then roll under the palms of the hands, upon the molding board, until each is five or six inches in length—rolling at last upon the ends only, so as to make them pointed and smaller. Place two of these rolls together, and lifting one end of each roll upon the other, pinch together, lay in a flat, broad pan to rise, and brush over with melted butter. Leave half an inch space between the rolls so the crust of each roll may be perfect, and, when sufficiently light, bake in the pan in which they were put to rise.

French Rolls No. 3.—Divide sufficient dough for a small loaf into twelve pieces. With the finger-tips knead each piece into a ball, and place these balls an inch apart, on a greased baking pan or floured board, to rise. Brush over with melted butter, and let stand half an hour at a temperature of seventy-five degrees, then take each ball separately, and, with a rolling-pin not larger than one's finger, press in the center of each roll, pushing the dough each way from the center, until the dough under the rolling-pin is very thin and about an inch and a half in width. Lift up this double roll, stretch it until about an inch and a half longer, and lay it face downward upon a towel or cloth spread in a shallow pan, and close up against one side of the pan. Manipulate another of the rolls in the same manner and place beside the first, drawing up a portion of the towel between the rolls. Repeat the operation until all the rolls are in the pan. Let rise in this position half an hour, or until the rolls are very light, then lift carefully and place on a baking sheet or pan, face up, not allowing them to touch each other, and bake.

Crescents.—Roll the dough as directed for French Rolls No. 2, but twice as long, which will leave it only half as large. Roll down at the ends to make them pointed. Place two of these long, slender rolls beside each other, and throwing them alternately over each other, twist them together, and pinch the ends close. Put them on a baking sheet or pan in the form of a crescent or horse shoe, and let them rise for an hour, or until light, then bake.

Queen Ann Rolls.—Shape the dough as for French rolls, twist two of the rolls together as for crescents, lay in Queen Ann pans or large roll-pans, let stand an hour, or until light, then bake.

Rolls of all kinds are more crisp and tender when baked quickly, and the oven should be hotter for rolls than for bread. They should also be considerably lighter than bread when put to bake, as they have but little opportunity to rise after they go in the oven, if it is hot enough to bake them properly. If a thick crust is desired they should remain in the oven a longer time.

LESSON VIII.—MIXING.

Arrangement of Lesson.

1. Give instruction concerning baking powder, its action in making batter and dough light.
2. Make wheat muffins with baking powder and milk.
3. Have several pupils make wheat muffins.
4. Make wheat muffins with sour milk and soda. Explain the action of soda.
5. Have several pupils make Wheat Muffins No. 2.
6. Make griddle cakes with sweet milk, baking powder, and eggs.
7. Have pupils make griddle cakes with sweet milk, baking powder, and eggs.
8. Have pupils make griddle cakes with sour milk and soda.

Formulas for Lesson VIII.

Wheat Muffins No. 1.—Two cups of flour, one cup of sweet milk, two tablespoonfuls of melted butter, two tablespoonfuls of baking powder, a pinch of salt. Sift the baking powder and salt with the flour into the mixing bowl, add the milk, and beat well, then add the melted butter. Bake half an hour.

Wheat Muffins No. 2.—One and one half cups of flour, one cup of thick sour milk, one half teaspoonful of soda, a pinch of salt. Sift the soda, salt, and flour together, add the milk, stir lightly, and bake.

Wheat Griddle Cakes No. 1.—One and a half cups of flour, one cup of sweet milk, two level teaspoonfuls of baking powder, one tablespoonful of melted butter, one egg, a pinch of salt. Sift the baking powder, salt, and flour together into the mixing bowl, add the milk, butter, and yolk of egg, beat until very light, then fold in the white of the egg beaten stiff, and bake in cakes on a hot griddle.

Wheat Griddle Cakes No. 2.—One rounded cup of flour, one cup of thick, sour milk, one teaspoonful of soda, a pinch of salt. Sift the soda, salt, and flour together into the mixing bowl, add the sour milk, and stir with a spoon, but only until thoroughly mixed. Bake on a griddle.

LESSON IX.—MIXING.

Arrangement of Lesson.

1. Make baking powder biscuit.
2. Have pupils make baking powder biscuit.
3. Make scrap meat pie.
4. Give instruction concerning corn-meal, illustrated by the prepared analysis; also upon the proper way of handling corn-meal.[1]
5. Make corn-meal muffins.
6. Have pupils make corn-meal muffins.
7. Make corn-bread.
8. Have pupils make corn-bread.
9. Make corn griddle cakes.
10. Have pupils make corn griddle cakes.

Formulas for Lesson IX.

Baking Powder Biscuit.—Two cups of flour, one

---
[1] "The Art of Cookery," pp. 207-209.

cup of sweet milk, two teaspoonfuls of baking powder, one half teaspoonful of salt. Sift the salt, baking powder, and flour together, add the milk, and beat to a smooth dough. Turn upon a well-floured molding board, dust with flour, and roll into a sheet about an inch in thickness. Dip the biscuit cutter in flour, cut the sheet of dough into cakes, lay in a baking pan, and bake in a quick oven until thoroughly done.

Scrap Meat Pie.—Fill a baking dish three quarters full with odds and ends of cold cooked meat—chicken, beef, veal, lamb, etc.—from which the skin, gristle, and objectionable bones have been removed. Cook together in a sauce-pan one tablespoonful of butter and two tablespoonfuls of flour, add two cups of soup stock, simmer five minutes or until smooth, season to taste, and pour over the prepared scrap meat in the pie. Cover loosely with a crust rolled to one quarter inch in thickness and bake until the crust is cooked.

Corn-meal.—The roller mill has worked as great an improvement in corn-meal as it has in flour, and the corn-meal of to-day is vastly superior in quality to the corn-meal of twenty-five years ago, and requires very different handling. And yet the recipes given in most cook-books prescribe "one cup of wheat flour and two cups of corn-meal," or else "two cups of wheat flour and one cup of corn-meal," for making all kinds of corn-bread. These are the formulas that were in vogue when bolted corn-meal was the only meal manufactured and used, and if they produced satisfactory results with bolted meal, they certainly do not when granulated meal is used. Such a mixture—whether the meal be bolted or granulated—does not make bread of any kind of a very high character; but, be its character high or low, it has no legitimate claim to the title of corn-bread. For bread-making purposes wheat flour and corn-meal have no affinity whatever, as one requires scalding and the other does not.

Corn-meal requires a good deal of cooking to develop its finest flavor, and make it palatable and healthful; and the main point in making good corn-bread is to scald the meal thoroughly. The water used for scalding meal should be boiling, and that none of its efficacy be lost it is desirable that the vessel in which the dough is mixed, and the spoon with which it is stirred, should be warm. There is a vast difference in the quality of corn-bread made with scalded meal and that made with meal which has been merely soaked with warm water. Almost every kind of corn-bread is better for being cooked from forty to sixty minutes, and if the meal is not thoroughly scalded when mixed it should be baked considerably longer. Granulated meal makes much lighter, drier, sweeter, and more delicious bread than bolted meal, and is preferable for all culinary purposes. But it should be always thoroughly scalded with boiling water or milk before it is made into bread or cakes, and whenever cold milk is used it should be added gradually. There are several grades of granulated meal—some being quite coarse and some very fine—and as the coarse will absorb fully twice as much water as the fine in the process of scalding, it requires the exercise of judgment to have the dough of the proper consistency—neither too soft nor too stiff. The formulas here given are for meal of medium fineness. If the meal used is very coarse more liquid will be required, if very fine less liquid.

Corn Muffins.—One cup of granulated corn-meal, three fourths of a cup of boiling water, one half cup of cold sweet milk, one heaping teaspoonful of sugar, one level teaspoonful of salt, one egg. Mix the sugar and salt with the meal, scald with the boiling water, add the cold milk gradually, stir in the egg, and bake in muffin cups, or in shallow pie-pans.

Corn-Bread.—One cup of granulated corn-meal, one and one quarter cups of boiling milk, one tablespoonful of butter, one heaping teaspoonful of sugar, one level teaspoonful of salt, two eggs. Mix the meal, salt, and sugar together, scald with boiling milk, add the butter, and, when the mixture is sufficiently cool, stir in the yolks and whites of the eggs, beaten separately. Bake in loaves.

Corn Griddle Cakes.—One cup of granulated corn-meal, three fourths of a cup of boiling water, half a cup of cold sweet milk, one heaping teaspoonful of sugar, one level teaspoonful of salt, one tablespoonful of flour, one teaspoonful of baking powder, one egg. Mix the sugar and salt with the meal, scald with the boiling water, stir in the egg, add the flour and baking powder, beat well, and bake in small cakes on the griddle. Cakes made of corn-meal require longer cooking than those made of wheat flour.

LESSON X.—MIXING AND SEASONING.

Soup and Puddings.

ARRANGEMENT OF LESSON.

1. Have pupils prepare and cook vegetables for vegetable soup—stock prepared.
2. Make caramel sauce.
3. Make Bread and Butter Pudding No. 1.
4. Have pupils make Bread and Butter Pudding No. 1.
5. Have pupils make Bread and Butter Pudding No. 2.
6. Have pupils make Bread and Butter Pudding No. 3.
7. Have pupils make baked apple pudding.
8. Make liquid sauce.
9. Make creamed butter and sugar.

FORMULAS FOR LESSON X.

Vegetable Soup.—Cook half a cup each of carrots, turnips, and onions chopped fine. Add four cups of beef stock, half a cup of diced tomato, and one tablespoonful of minced parsley. Simmer fifteen minutes, season to taste, and serve.

Caramel Sauce.—To one cup of granulated sugar add half a cup of water, and boil until the mixture begins to color, then cook slowly, and stir, if necessary, to produce an even or uniform coloring. When of a bright chestnut brown, add half a cup of hot water, cook five minutes, and serve either hot or cold.

Bread and Butter Pudding No. 1.—Butter slices of stale bread thinly on both sides, and cover the bottom of a shallow baking dish with them. Pour as much sweet milk over the bread as it will absorb, then pour over it a custard made from two cups of rich milk, a pinch of salt, and four well-beaten eggs. Bake in a moderate oven until firm in the center and nicely browned over the surface. Serve hot, with creamed butter and sugar, liquid or caramel sauce.

Bread and Butter Pudding No. 2.—Prepare and bake like Bread and Butter Pudding No. 1, but add four tablespoonfuls of sugar to the custard. Dust with mace or nutmeg, and serve cold.

Bread and Butter Pudding No. 3.—Prepare and bake like Bread and Butter Pudding No. 1, but use half a cup of caramel sauce to sweeten the pudding.

Baked Apple Pudding.—Cover the bottom of a buttered pudding dish with quarters of sour apples that have been pared and cored. Dust lightly with salt, and lay over them slices of stale bread that have been soaked in cold water until thoroughly saturated. Place a layer of quarters of apples upon the moist bread and cover thickly with soft fine bread crumbs, moistened lightly with melted butter. Sift two tablespoonfuls of granulated sugar over the apples, cover with a buttered pie-pan or tin cover, and bake in a moderate oven for half an hour, or until the apples are soft, then remove the cover, let the pudding brown, and serve warm with creamed butter and sugar, or liquid sauce.

Liquid Sauce.—Mix together a tablespoonful of flour and a cup of granulated sugar, add a cup of boiling water, and simmer five minutes. Add a fourth of a teaspoonful of grated nutmeg, and lastly whip into the mixture half a cup of butter, beaten to a cream.

Creamed Butter and Sugar.—Put half a cup of butter into a pint bowl, slightly warmed, and stir with a wooden spoon until it is soft and creamy, then add, a tablespoonful at a time, one cup of pulverized sugar—stirring the mixture after adding each spoonful of sugar. Flavor with one teaspoonful of vanilla extract, and add also, if desired, two or three tablespoonfuls of sweet cream—a tablespoonful at a time, beating well before adding more.

LESSON XI.—SALADS.

Arrangement of Lesson.

1. Have pupils prepare and cook cabbage.
2. Make sauce hollandaise.
3. Make cabbage salad. Have pupils prepare and cut the cabbage.
4. Have pupils make cooked mayonnaise dressing.
5. Make onion salad.
6. Have pupils make cream dressing.
7. Make potato salad. Boil potatoes in the skin, calling attention to the advantage of this manner of cooking potatoes.

Formulas for Lesson XI.

Sauce Hollandaise.—Cook together until well mixed one tablespoonful each of butter and flour, add a cup of sweet milk or cream, simmer five minutes, then stir in the yolks of three eggs, well beaten, with a tablespoonful of water. Add the eggs slowly and continue the cooking, after the egg is all in, for about a minute. Remove from the fire, add a tablespoonful of butter and one of lemon juice, and season with salt and pepper.

Cabbage Salad.—Soak the prepared cabbage in cold water till crisp. Shave thin, and dress with cooked mayonnaise.

Cooked Mayonnaise Dressing.—Pour four tablespoonfuls of boiling vinegar over two whole eggs, or the yolks of four eggs, which have been well beaten, stirring the mixture while adding the vinegar. Put in a small sauce-pan over the fire, and cook slowly, stirring constantly, until the mixture is thick and creamy. Remove from the fire, add a tablespoonful of butter, and stir until perfectly mixed. Season to taste with sugar, salt, and pepper.

Onion Salad.—Remove the skin from a medium-sized onion, slice as thin as possible, put on broken ice, and when chilled and crisp serve with a dressing made from mixing together one teaspoonful of sugar, one half teaspoonful of salt, one eighth of a teaspoonful of white pepper, and two teaspoonfuls of sharp vinegar.

Cream Dressing.—Cook together two tablespoonfuls each of butter and flour, add a cup of thin cream, and simmer five minutes. Then add gradually four tablespoonfuls of vinegar. When perfectly cold beat in one cup of whipped cream, or one half cup of thin cream. Add one tablespoonful each of minced onion and parsley, and season to taste with salt and pepper.

Potato Salad.—Pour cream dressing over thinly sliced cold boiled potatoes.

LESSON XII.—A LUNCHEON.

Have pupils prepare and serve a luncheon under supervision of teacher, confining the bill of fare to such dishes as the pupils have learned to prepare and cook. This lesson should be a test of proficiency.

SECOND TERM.

LESSON I.—BROILING.

Arrangement of Lesson.

1. Prepare chicken for broiling; give instruction in best method of cleaning and dressing poultry [1]; also in selecting poultry.[2]
2. Give instruction in oven broiling.[3]
3. Prepare a fish for broiling.
4. Broil fish in oven.
5. Have pupils make dry toast.
6. Have pupils make dipped toast.
7. Have pupils make cream toast.
8. Prepare parsley butter for fish.
9. Carve fish.
10. Carve chicken.
11. Broil oysters.
12. Broil oysters on griddle.

Have pupils do the work after instruction in preparing oysters for broiling.

Formulas for Lesson I.

To Pick a Fowl.—Fowls that are picked dry are considered superior to those whose feathers are removed

---

[1] "The Art of Cookery," pp. 20–21.
[2] "The Art of Cookery," p. 13.
[3] "The Art of Cookery," p. 43.

by scalding, but as the latter method is the one in general use and is much easier and quicker than dry picking, it is the method here given : Hold the fowl by the feet or legs, plunge it in very hot water, and draw it out again almost instantly. Repeat the process several times, until the feathers are thoroughly soaked and can be pulled out easily. Then take the fowl in the left hand, and with the right hand pluck out the feathers, stripping them from the legs down toward the head. After all the feathers have been removed, rub out the pin feathers with a coarse cloth, and singe off the hairs over a blaze of alcohol or gas.

To Draw a Fowl.—Cut off the head of the fowl, if it has not already been removed. Slit the skin the full length of the neck at the back, and carefully loosen it from the neck and craw. Cut off the neck about an inch from the body, and remove the craw and windpipe, being careful not to tear the skin of the fowl. Insert a sharp-pointed knife in front of, and close to, the tail and cut through the skin around the vent and outside the entrail. Lift up the skin below the breast-bone of the fowl, leaving a strip an inch in width above the vent. Cut crosswise two inches and make an opening large enough to insert two fingers, with which carefully draw out the entire contents of the body of the fowl. Separate the heart, liver, and gizzard from the entrails. Remove the gall-sack from the liver very carefully, and open and empty the gizzard.

To Draw a Bird.—This is the best and easiest way of drawing a bird or young chicken that is to be broiled : Insert a small sharp-pointed knife between the shoulder and the back-bone and cut down the back the entire length of the fowl or bird—being careful not to cut into the entrails. Lay the fowl or bird open and remove the contents of the body.

To Wash a Fowl.—Dissolve a teaspoonful of soda in two quarts of water, and with a cloth or brush wash the skin of the fowl very thoroughly. Rinse the inside with the soda water. Wash the giblets also. Rinse all in cold water and wipe dry with a soft towel.

To Broil a Chicken in the Oven.—After the chicken has been split down the back and properly prepared, lay it inside down upon a meat-board and press the joints and breast-bone close to the board with a rolling-pin—crushing them down until the chicken is quite flat—then wipe off all moisture with a dry towel, and lay the flattened chicken inside down upon a smoking hot roasting pan. Put a weight upon it to keep it pressed close to the pan until well seared and lightly browned. After the searing and browning have been accomplished remove the weight, and put the chicken, without taking it from the pan, into a very hot oven. Place it on the upper grate so the greatest heat may be from above. Close the oven door and leave the chicken undisturbed for twenty minutes. At the end of that time it will be evenly browned on the outside, and, if young and not large, will be perfectly cooked all through. If full grown or very large it will have to be cooked from forty to sixty minutes. When cooked, lay upon a platter, season with salt, pepper, and melted butter, and serve.

To Broil a Fish in the Oven.—Open the fish down the front, lay it, skin side down, on a fish rack, or on oiled paper, in a roasting pan, season with salt, pepper, and melted butter, and dust with flour. Put to cook on the upper grate of a hot oven, and, when nicely browned, place on a warm platter, season with plain or parsley butter, and serve. A fish weighing three or four pounds will broil in an oven at the right temperature in about half an hour, and one of larger size in a proportionately greater length of time.

Dipped Toast.—Put a cup of boiling water, a tablespoonful of butter, and a fourth of a teaspoonful of salt, in a shallow basin, on the back of the stove. Dip the toasted bread, a slice at a time, into the mixture, turn it over with a knife and fork, and lift on to a heated platter before it becomes too soft. If the toast is required richer, more butter may be used. Hot milk may also be used in place of water, if preferred.

Creamed Toast.—Put in a shallow pan or basin on the back of the stove a cup of milk, a tablespoonful of butter, and a fourth of a teaspoonful of salt. Mix well together and dip the toasted bread, by laying a slice at a time in the hot mixture. With a fork and a limber-bladed knife turn it over, press under the milk, and lift at once into a warm tureen. After all the toast wanted has been dipped and lifted to the tureen in this manner, pour over it a cup of white sauce.

White Sauce.—Cook together one tablespoonful of butter and one of flour, add one cup of cream, simmer five minutes, season, and serve.

Parsley Butter.—To one tablespoonful of butter add a teaspoonful of minced parsley and a teaspoonful of lemon juice. Season with salt and pepper and mix well.

To Broil Oysters.—Roll the oysters in fine bread crumbs, dip in melted butter, lay in a wire broiler, and cook quickly over a brisk fire, turning the broiler as often as necessary.

To Broil Oysters on a Griddle.—Drain the oysters in a colander or sieve, dip each oyster in melted butter that has been clarified, and lay upon a plate for convenient handling. Have a griddle clean, smoking hot, and perfectly dry. Fill it quickly with the buttered oysters, laying them closely together upon it. By the time the griddle is filled, if the fire is sufficiently hot, the oysters first laid upon it will be browned and broiled. With a limber knife and a fork turn the oysters upon the griddle, in the order in which they were laid upon it. As soon as they are turned begin removing those first put upon the griddle, and so proceed until they are all lifted upon a warm platter on which salt, pepper, and butter have been placed. Or they can be laid upon thin slices of toast and seasoned with salt, pepper, and melted butter.

LESSON II.—ROASTING AND STEWING.

ARRANGEMENT OF LESSON.

1. Prepare stuffing and stuff a chicken. (Have chicken already dressed.)
2. Prepare and stuff pork for roasting.

3. Stew cranberries.
4. Have pupils stew apples.
5. Have pupils brown white potatoes.
6. Have pupils brown sweet potatoes.
7. Have pupils make chicken gravy.
8. Have pupils make gravy for roast pork.
9. Carve the chicken.[1]

Formulas for Lesson II.

Stuffing for Poultry.—To prepare crumbs for stuffing meats, poultry, etc., remove the crust from a loaf of stale bread, break the loaf in the middle, and rub the jagged or rough edges against each other until the bread is rubbed into tolerably fine crumbs. Season to taste with salt and pepper the desired quantity of crumbs, and moisten lightly with melted butter. If additional seasoning be desired, minced parsley, celery, or onion may be used.

To Roast a Chicken.—Place the chicken, after it has been properly cleaned, in a large bowl, tail downward, put the prepared crumbs in at the neck until the breast becomes plump, then draw the skin together, and fasten over on the back. Reverse the position of the chicken in the bowl, put the remaining crumbs in the body, at the opening through which the entrails were removed, and sew it up with strong thread. Press the wings and legs as close to the body as possible, and secure them firmly in position with strings or skewers. Lay the chicken, breast downward, on a rack in the roasting

[1] "The Art of Cookery," p. 316.

pan, and let it remain in that position until the back is a light brown color, then turn it over, and let the breast and sides brown in a similar manner. Do not put any water in the pan during this process. When the entire chicken is nicely browned begin basting with a thin gravy. As this basting gravy evaporates, add a little boiling water to keep it from burning in the pan, and baste as often as the skin of the chicken becomes dry, until the roasting is completed. The time required for roasting a chicken varies according to its size and age. But an hour and a half is sufficient time to allow for a large, full-grown chicken not over a year old.

Stuffing for Pork.—Season to taste with salt and pepper the desired quantity of bread crumbs, add a little sage or sweet marjoram, and moisten with melted butter.

To Roast Fresh Pork.—Make pockets under the skin and fill them with the stuffing, or pack it upon the inside of the roast, roll up tightly, pin with skewers, tie securely with twine, place upon a rack in the roasting pan, and put in the oven. As soon as it is a light brown color baste with hot water seasoned with salt and pepper, and renew the operation every fifteen minutes until the roast is thoroughly cooked. It requires fully twice as long a time to roast pork as it does to roast beef or mutton, and as the frequent bastings keep it from becoming hardened, a piece of pork weighing not more than three or four pounds can be roasted with advantage two or two and a half hours.

To Stew Cranberries.—To a quart of cranberries

picked and washed add three fourths of a pint of boiling water, cover closely, and cook five minutes over a quick fire. Mash with a wooden spoon such of the berries as have not burst, and rub through a colander or pumpkin strainer into an earthen dish or bowl. Put the pulp into the sauce-pan in which the berries were cooked, add three fourths of a pint of granulated sugar, simmer five minutes, and serve hot or cold. When cold the sauce will be jellied.

Browned White Potatoes.—Pare the potatoes, and parboil them for fifteen minutes. Put into a baking pan some gravy from the roast pork. Roll the potatoes in the gravy till well coated, then put them into the oven till thoroughly cooked and nicely browned.

Browned Sweet Potatoes.—Wash the potatoes and boil until tender. Drain, pare the potatoes, and roll them in melted butter. Then put them into a baking pan and brown them nicely in the oven.

Chicken Gravy; Gravy for Roast Pork.—See Roast Beef Gravy, Lesson III., Term I.

LESSON III.—BOILING.

ARRANGEMENT OF LESSON.

1. Boil a fowl whole (fowl prepared).
2. Steam graham pudding.
3. Have pupils prepare and stew onions.
4. Have pupils boil rice.
5. Have pupils make celery sauce.
6. Have pupils make drawn butter sauce.

7. Have pupils make parsley sauce.
8. Have pupils make oyster sauce.
9. Make liquid sauce for pudding. (Demonstration by pupil.)
10. Have a pupil carve the chicken.

Formulas for Lesson III.

To Boil a Fowl.—Truss the legs and wings close to the body. Put into a kettle of boiling, salted water—being careful to have enough water to submerge completely the fowl—and cook until the skin assumes a gelatinous appearance and the fowl becomes tender. When done take out, carefully remove all the trussing strings and skewers, and lay on a platter. Serve with parsley, oyster, or celery sauce.

Graham Pudding.—Three cups of graham flour, one cup of sweet milk, one cup of molasses, one cup of raisins, one teaspoonful of salt, three teaspoonfuls of baking powder. Mix the dry ingredients and raisins together, then add the molasses and milk. Steam in a buttered mold four hours.

To Clean Raisins.—Pour boiling water over them, let them stand five minutes, rub dry. Tear in two and eject the seeds.

To Stew Onions.—Peel, boil half an hour, drain, cover with milk, stew until tender, drain, mash or chop, add a little cream, stir over the fire until thoroughly heated, then season with salt and pepper; or when cooked tender dress with salt, pepper, and butter, and serve whole.

Celery Sauce.—To one cup of drawn butter made with celery stock add one cup of white celery, cut in dice, and cooked tender. Simmer five minutes, season, and serve with boiled or roasted turkey, chicken, or veal.

Celery Stock.—Put the roots and coarse outside pieces of half a dozen stalks of celery into three pints of slightly salted water, simmer an hour, strain, and use for stock.

Drawn Butter Sauce.—Make drawn butter sauce as in Lesson IV., Term I., using chicken broth instead of mutton broth.

Parsley Sauce.—Cook together a tablespoonful each of butter and flour, add a cup of chicken broth and a teaspoonful of minced parsley. Simmer five minutes, add another teaspoonful of butter, season, and serve with boiled chicken.

Oyster Sauce.—To one cup of drawn butter made with water add a dozen medium-sized oysters and simmer five minutes, or until the thin edges wrinkle and separate. Season and serve with boiled codfish, boiled turkey, capon, or fowl.

Liquid Sauce.—See Lesson X., Term I.

LESSON IV.—STEAMING AND STEWING.

Arrangement of Lesson.

1. Prepare and put to stew veal for a pot pie.
2. Give instruction in making cream soups.
3. Have pupils prepare and cook potatoes for cream of potato soup.

4. Have pupils prepare and cook celery for cream of celery soup.
5. Make cream of tomato soup.
6. Have pupils finish their soups.
7. Have pupils make dumplings for pot pie.
8. Serve soups while the dumplings are steaming.
9. Serve the pot pie.

FORMULAS FOR LESSON IV.

Veal Pot Pie.—Select thin portions of veal in which the lean and fat are about equally combined. Remove the outer skin, cut the meat in pieces suitable for serving, put it into a stew-pan, add a teaspoonful of salt and hot water enough barely to cover the meat. Cover the stew-pan closely, and let the meat cook slowly for two or three hours. Add the dumplings, and steam for fifteen or twenty minutes without lifting the cover. Remove the meat and dumplings, and thicken the broth with a tablespoonful each of butter and flour, stirred to a smooth paste.

Dumplings.—One and three quarters cups of flour, one cup of sweet milk, two teaspoonfuls of baking powder, one half teaspoonful of salt. Sift the salt, baking powder, and flour together, add the milk, and beat to a smooth dough. Place a spoonful of dough upon each piece of meat, being careful that it does not sink into the broth.

Cream of Potato Soup.—Cook together one tablespoonful of butter and two tablespoonfuls of flour. Add a cup and a half of boiled mashed potato and half a cup of boiled mashed onion and two cups of hot water. Rub through a sieve and return to the sauce-pan. Add a cupful of thin cream, heat to boiling point, and season to taste.

Cream of Celery Soup.—Cook together in a sauce-pan until well mixed one tablespoonful of butter and two tablespoonfuls of flour, add four cups of celery stock, and simmer five minutes. Pour in a cup of sweet cream, heat to boiling point, season to taste.

Cream of Tomato Soup.—To one tablespoonful of butter and two tablespoonfuls of flour cooked together add three cupfuls of strained tomato. Simmer five minutes. Add one cupful of cream, and season to taste.

LESSON V.—FRYING.

Arrangement of Lesson.

1. Have pupils prepare potatoes and fish for fish balls and fish cakes.
2. Have a number of the pupils make the potatoes and fish into fish balls and fry them.
3. Have the remainder make fish cakes and sauté them.
4. Have pupils sauté potatoes.
5. Have pupils sauté apples.
6. Fry oysters.
7. Sauté oysters.
8. Make lyonnaise potatoes.

Formulas for Lesson V.

Codfish Balls.—To a cup of salt codfish, cut in small pieces, freed from skin and bone, and well washed in cold water, add a cup of raw potato also cut in small pieces. Put in a sauce-pan, cover with boiling water, and simmer gently until the potato is cooked. Then drain, dry off carefully, mash the codfish and potato together, add a dust of white pepper, a tablespoonful of sweet milk, a teaspoonful of butter, and the unbeaten whites of two eggs, or one whole egg. Fry in spoonfuls in hot fat, drain on cheese-cloth, and serve with poached eggs on toast.

To Saute Fish Cakes.—Mix together half a pint of boiled codfish freed from bones and skin, half a pint of mashed, boiled potato, two tablespoonfuls of sweet milk, and one tablespoonful of butter. Season to taste with salt and pepper, form into cakes half an inch thick, and brown in a spider in hot butter, or the drippings of salt pork or breakfast bacon.

To Saute Potatoes.—Slice cold boiled potatoes in slices a sixteenth of an inch in thickness, season to taste with salt and pepper, and brown on both sides in clarified butter. Serve in a warm, covered dish, or as a garnish to beefsteak or chops of any kind.

To Saute Apples.—Wash and wipe sour apples, remove the blossom end and all blemishes of skin, slice in rounds a sixteenth of an inch thick, dust with flour, and cook in clarified butter in a spider till brown on both sides. If the slices are not soft when brown, cover the spider and let them simmer a few minutes on a cooler part of the range. Serve with broiled ham, breakfast bacon, pork chops, or tenderloin.

To Fry Oysters.—Select large oysters, drain on a

sieve, lay singly on a plate, and season with salt and pepper. Lift each oyster by sticking a small skewer through its thin edge, dip it in white corn-meal and flour sifted together in equal proportions, cover with egg batter, then with crumbs, fry in a basket in very hot fat, drain on cheese-cloth, and serve on a warm platter.

To Saute Oysters.—Drain the oysters in a colander or on a sieve, season with salt and pepper, roll in white corn-meal or crumbs, and brown quickly in a little clarified butter in a spider. Serve on a warm platter.

Lyonnaise Potato.—Put two tablespoonfuls of clarified butter in a skillet or frying pan, and when melted add to it two tablespoonfuls of minced onion. Cook till the onion turns yellow, then add two cups of diced or hashed cold potato, with which a tablespoonful of minced parsley has been mixed, and which has been seasoned with salt and pepper. Cover and cook slowly until nicely browned on the under side, then fold like an omelet, and serve on a heated dish. If the cold potato is very dry two or three spoonfuls of sweet milk may be mixed with it before the parsley and seasoning are added.

LESSON VI.—MIXING.

Scalloped Meats and Vegetables.

ARRANGEMENT OF LESSON.

1. Have pupils prepare and cook macaroni.
2. Prepare and scallop raw potatoes.

3. Scallop cold cooked potatoes.
4. Scallop chicken or veal.
5. Scallop oysters.
6. Scallop macaroni.

FORMULAS FOR LESSON VI.

To Boil Macaroni.—See Lesson V., Term I.

Scalloped Potatoes No. 1.—Pare and slice the potatoes of a uniform thickness. Butter a baking dish and fill three quarters full with the prepared potatoes. Add milk until the potatoes are nearly covered, season to taste with salt and pepper, then sprinkle generously with bread crumbs, rolled and sifted. Bake in a moderate oven for half an hour, or until the potatoes are cooked and the crumbs browned.

Scalloped Potatoes No. 2.—To three cups of cold boiled or baked potatoes cut into dice, sliced, or hashed, add a teaspoonful of minced parsley and a cup of white sauce made from cooking together one tablespoonful of butter, one teaspoonful of flour, and one cup of milk. Put in a buttered baking dish, cover with bread crumbs, and brown in the oven.

Scalloped Chicken.—Free the cold chicken, either roasted, boiled, or fried, from skin and tough or sinewy bits, and cut in small pieces. To two cups of prepared chicken add one cup of white sauce, made from cooking together one tablespoonful of butter, one teaspoonful of flour, and one cup of thin cream. Cover with buttered bread crumbs and bake until the crumbs are nicely browned.

Scalloped Oysters.—Drain a quart of oysters. To a pint of soft fine bread crumbs add salt and pepper sufficient to season the oysters properly. Mix the seasoning uniformly through the crumbs with a fork. Then enrich them by sprinkling through, and mixing with them, half a cup of melted butter. Take a fireproof dish or baking pan not more than two inches deep, in which to cook the oysters. Scatter a thin layer of the seasoned crumbs over the bottom of the dish. Cover the crumbs with oysters, laying the oysters close together, but not overlapping each other. Sprinkle with the crumbs until nearly hidden from view, then add another layer of oysters and again sprinkle with crumbs. The top layer of crumbs should be heavier than either of the other layers—should contain fully one half the quantity of crumbs used—and but two layers of oysters should be put in the dish. Do not pour oyster juice, water, or liquid of any kind over the oysters after they are put in the dish. Bake in an oven, at the same temperature as for bread, for fifteen or twenty minutes, or until the crumbs on top are a rich chestnut brown. Remove from the oven as soon as cooked and serve at once, and the oysters will be plump, juicy, hot to the center, and surrounded by a delicious, moist coating of crumbs.

Scalloped Macaroni.—To three or four cups of boiled, drained macaroni add one cup of thin white sauce and one tablespoonful of grated cheese. Cover with a layer of buttered bread crumbs and brown in a moderate oven.

LESSON VII.—MIXING.

Pastry and Pies.

ARRANGEMENT OF LESSON.

1. Make flaky pie crust. Explain the enfolding of air between the layers of the pastry to give it lightness. Give careful instruction in mixing and rolling; also in the difference between bread and pastry flour.
2. Have each pupil make flaky pie crust.
3. Have a number of pupils prepare lemon filling for pie.
4. Have several pupils make custard for pie.
5. Have the remainder prepare apples for pie.
6. Bake the pies. Give instruction as to temperature of oven, etc.
7. Have all make cheese straws from remnants of pie crust.

FORMULAS FOR LESSON VII.

Flaky Pie Crust.—Three cups of flour, half a cup of butter, half a cup of lard, three fourths of a cup of ice water.

Sift the flour into a chopping bowl, add the butter and lard, and chop with a hash knife until no pieces of the shortening larger than a pea can be seen. Then sprinkle the ice water here and there through the flour, and mix with a fork into a rather soft dough or paste. Pile upon a well-floured kneading board, dust lightly with flour, press down with the rolling-pin, and roll gently back and forth until the paste becomes an oblong sheet not more than half an inch in thickness. Slip a broad-bladed knife under each end of this sheet, and fold over toward the center, thus forming three layers of the paste. Lift, with the knife, from the board—which dust with fresh flour—lay it at right angles with the position it occupied when lifted, dust with flour, roll out, and again fold over as before. Repeat the operation, and the paste is ready to lay aside for future use, or to roll into form and use at once.

Lemon Pie.—Two cups of boiling water, a cup and a half of sugar, half a cup of lemon juice, a tablespoonful of butter, a tablespoonful of cornstarch, grated peel of a lemon, three eggs. Mix the sugar and cornstarch well together, add them to the boiling water, and cook five minutes. Remove from the fire, add the butter, lemon juice and peel, and lastly the eggs, beaten very light. Line a deep pie-pan with paste, dust with flour, fill three fourths full with the mixture, and bake in a moderate oven till firm in the center. When cold sift powdered sugar over it and serve.

Custard Pie.—To half a cup of granulated sugar add one tablespoonful of cornstarch, mix well, stir it into two cups of milk, boiling hot, and simmer five minutes. When cool add three well-beaten eggs and a pinch of salt. Line a deep pie-pan with paste, dust with flour, and fill three quarters full with the mixture. Bake in a moderate oven until firm in the center. Grate nutmeg over the top and serve cool.

Apple Pie.—Roll a piece of flaky pie crust to the thickness desired. Place upon a pie-pan or dish, shaping it carefully to the dish, and cut off around the edges with a sharp knife. Cover the bottom of the crust with a thin layer of sugar, dust with flour, then fill the crust with quarters of pared and cored apples. Dust them lightly with salt and generously with sugar—especially if they are very tart—roll an upper crust and lay over them, trim around the edges as before, press the upper and lower crusts together lightly, and bake half an hour, or until the apples are soft and the top and bottom crusts are both nicely browned.

Cheese Straws.—Roll the same thickness as for pies. When rolled, cut in strips from six to ten inches wide, and cut the strips into straws or sticks a fourth of an inch in width. Lay upon baking sheets or shallow pans, leaving a space between the straws about a third as wide as the straws. Grate rich American cheese, season to taste with salt and red pepper, and scatter quite thickly over the straws, and over the spaces between them also. Place in the oven where the greatest heat will be at the top, and bake ten or fifteen minutes, or until cooked. Remove from the oven, cut the cheese in the center of the spaces between the straws, and pile the straws on a plate in the form of a log cabin.

LESSON VIII.—MIXING.

Bread and Buns.

ARRANGEMENT OF LESSON.

1. Make cinnamon rolls from light bun dough.
2. Make coffee cake from light dough.

3. Make into loaves light dough mixed from graham flour.
4. Make into loaves light dough from whole wheat flour. First and second divisions of work may be done successively; third and fourth may be done at the same time. Divide the work so that each pupil shall handle some of the dough.
5. Have a number of pupils mix bun dough.
6. Have the remainder mix either whole wheat bread or graham bread.
7. Give instruction concerning graham flour and entire wheat flour.
8. Bake the buns, coffee cake, and bread.

FORMULAS FOR LESSON VIII.

Cinnamon Rolls.—Roll small pieces of bun dough, after it has risen the second time, into small rolls or sticks. Flatten with a limber knife and cover with melted butter, sugar, and cinnamon. Fold over and roll into circular cakes with one end in the center, and the other pinched to the outer surface, and place in a baking pan, an inch apart. Let rise two hours, and bake in a moderate oven.

Coffee Cake.—Roll a piece of bun dough after it has risen the second time into a sheet half an inch thick, lay on a shallow baking pan, cover with granulated sugar, then with cinnamon, and lastly with melted butter. Let rise for two hours, or until very light, then bake in a moderate oven.

Graham Bread.—To each pint of lukewarm wetting

composed of equal portions of sweet milk and water add a tablespoonful of sugar, half a teaspoonful of salt, and a half-ounce cake of compressed yeast, dissolved in two tablespoonfuls of cold water. Then stir in with a wooden spoon a heaping quart of graham flour, or as much more as may be necessary to form a dough sufficiently stiff to be removed in a mass from the mixing bowl. Turn the dough on to the molding board, well sprinkled with white flour, and knead, adding white flour until the dough ceases to stick to the fingers or molding board. Then proceed exactly as for white flour bread, being careful not to make the dough as stiff as for white bread. Bread is made in the same manner from entire wheat, whole wheat, and peeled wheat flour. The sugar may be omitted from any of them, when desired. Graham bread requires to be baked a considerably longer time than white flour bread, as does also bread made of either whole wheat, entire wheat, or peeled wheat flour. Consequently the loaves should be smaller and should be baked at a somewhat lower temperature.

Buns.—Two eggs, two cups of boiling milk, half cup of sugar, half cup of butter, one cake of compressed yeast, flour enough to make a dough. Beat the eggs very light, pour over them, beating meanwhile, the boiling milk, then add the sugar and salt. Let the mixture cool until lukewarm, then add the yeast, dissolved in a little cold water, and stir in flour until a soft dough has been formed. Turn upon the molding board and knead in flour gradually until the dough becomes smooth and elastic, but not stiff enough for bread, then put in a greased bowl, and set to rise for five hours, or until light. When light work in the butter, but do not add any more flour, and let rise for an hour, or until light, then form into buns or balls the size desired, place in a greased pan about an inch apart, and again let rise for two hours, or until light, then bake in a moderate oven.

LESSON IX.—MIXING.

Cake and Cookies.

Arrangement of Lesson.

1. Make soft ginger cake.
2. Have pupils make ginger cake.
3. Make cup cake.
4. Have pupils make cup cake.
5. Make plain cookies.
6. Have pupils make cookies.
7. Make ginger wafers.
8. Have pupils make wafers.

Formulas for Lesson IX.

Soft Ginger Cake.—Quarter of a cup of butter, half a cup of sugar, half a cup of sour milk, one cup of New Orleans molasses, two eggs, one tablespoonful of ginger, one teaspoonful of cinnamon, one teaspoonful of soda, half a teaspoonful of salt, and three cups of flour. Sift the soda, salt, and spices with the flour. Cream the butter, add the sugar, then the milk, then the flour and molasses alternately. Beat well and bake in shallow pans in a moderate oven.

Plain Cup Cake.—One fourth cup of butter, one and one half cups of sugar, one cup of milk, two eggs, three cups of flour, three teaspoonfuls of baking powder. Cream the butter, add the sugar and eggs alternately, and beat well. Add the milk and the flour containing the baking powder alternately.

Plain Sugar Cookies.—One half cup of butter, one cup of sugar, one fourth cup of milk, one egg, two teaspoonfuls of baking powder. Cream the butter and sugar, add the egg, and beat well. Sift the baking powder with two cups of flour, add it and the milk alternately. Use flour enough to roll out.

Ginger Wafers.—One cup of butter, two cups of pulverized sugar, one cup of cold water, four cups of flour, ginger to taste. Cream the butter, add the sugar and ginger, then stir in the water and flour gradually and alternately. Spread the mixture as thin as possible on a cold greased baking sheet, and bake in a moderate oven. As soon as done cut quickly, and while hot, into squares or diamonds, and roll, if desired.

LESSON X.—MIXING AND SEASONING.

Salads.

ARRANGEMENT OF LESSON.

1. Make French dressing. Have two or three pupils work at the same time.

2. Make mayonnaise dressing.
3. Have pupils make cooked mayonnaise dressing.
4. Have pupils prepare lettuce and cucumbers for salad. Put on ice.
5. Prepare fish and make fish salad, using the cooked mayonnaise dressing.
6. Prepare chicken and celery and make chicken salad, pupils working with teacher.
7. Finish lettuce and cucumber salad.

FORMULAS FOR LESSON X.

French Dressing.—Put a tablespoonful of very sharp vinegar into a cup which has been iced or made cold, add salt and white pepper to taste, then add gradually, stirring meanwhile, three tablespoonfuls of olive oil. The salt should be almost as plain to the taste in the mixture as the vinegar.

Mayonnaise Dressing.—In making this dressing select for use a Dover egg-beater and a large bowl-shaped coffee cup, or a pint bowl with straight sides. Have both well cooled with ice, also a fresh egg and the oil to be used for the dressing. Put the yolk of the egg into the cup and beat it for a few seconds before adding any oil. Beat in the oil, a few drops at a time, until it shows that it is combining perfectly with the egg, then add more freely. When the mixture becomes too stiff to beat easily add, one at a time, two teaspoonfuls of lemon juice or vinegar, which will thin it. Beat in more oil until again very stiff, when thin with acid as before. By thus alternating the oil and acid, a quart or more of oil may be made into a light, thick, cream-colored dressing with only one egg yolk.

To Prepare Cucumbers.—Lay the cucumbers upon ice, or in cold water, until half an hour before serving, then pare and slice upon broken ice. Just before serving drain off the water.

To Prepare Lettuce.—Cut off the root and remove the outside leaves from each head. Then remove the other leaves one by one and place them in cold water. Rinse carefully, lay in a fine wire basket, and swing in a draft of air to dry off, or lay on a coarse towel and shake gently until dry.

Lettuce and Cucumber Salad.—Sprinkle the French dressing upon the lettuce leaves, turning them over and about carefully until each leaf is covered with the dressing. Then arrange them in the salad bowl with the cucumbers in alternate layers.

Fish Salad.—Pick into pieces suitable for serving any cold cooked fresh fish, freed from skin and bones. With two cups of prepared fish mix half a cup of cooked mayonnaise dressing.

Chicken Salad.—Put four cups of cooked chicken, freed from skin, bones, and coarse pieces, and cut into dice, in an earthen bowl, and pour over it half a cup of French dressing. Make with one spoonful of oil to three of vinegar. Set in a cold place for an hour, drain through a sieve, mix with it three cups of white, tender celery cut in dice, and add, and mix lightly through it, a cup of oil mayonnaise dressing. Place in the salad bowl—heaping in the center—spread half a cup of mayonnaise dressing over it, sprinkle a spoonful of capers upon the dressing, and garnish with curled celery and water cress; or with olives, lemon points, hard-boiled eggs, or lettuce.

LESSON XI.—MIXING.

Blanc-Mange and Custards.

ARRANGEMENT OF LESSON.

1. Make cornstarch blanc-mange.
2. Make farina blanc-mange (pupils).
3. Make creamed tapioca.
4. Make creamed sago.
5. Make baked tapioca pudding.
6. Make sea moss blanc-mange.
7. Make baked custard (pupils).
8. Make Boiled Custard No. 1 (pupils).
9. Make Boiled Custard No. 2 (pupils).

FORMULAS FOR LESSON XI.

Cornstarch Blanc-Mange.—To two cups of boiling milk add one fourth of a cup of cornstarch mixed with the same quantity of granulated sugar, and salt to taste. Cook ten minutes, add the well-beaten yolks of two eggs, continue the cooking a couple of minutes, then remove from the fire, beat into the mixture the whites of the eggs beaten stiff, and lastly add a teaspoonful of extract of vanilla. Cool in molds wet with cold water, and serve with cream.

Farina Blanc-Mange.—To five cups of boiling milk

add half a cup of farina—sprinkling it in slowly and stirring to prevent the formation of lumps—and a level teaspoonful of salt. Simmer gently half an hour, put in molds, and let cool. Serve with sugar and cream, or with fruit or boiled custard.

Creamed Tapioca.—Soak a cup of tapioca in two cups of cold water for several hours. Drain, and put it into two cups of boiling milk, with a cup of sugar and half a teaspoonful of salt. Simmer gently for fifteen minutes, or until the tapioca is transparent, then add two eggs beaten very light, cook until creamy, and when cool flavor with vanilla.

Creamed Sago.—To two cups of boiling milk add half a cup of sago by sprinkling in slowly and stirring it smooth. Add half a teaspoonful of salt and half a cup of sugar, and cook gently fifteen or twenty minutes. Beat the whites of two eggs to a stiff froth and put in a china bowl or dish. Beat the yolks with a tablespoonful of milk, and add to the pudding, and when cooked to a creamy consistency pour the boiling mixture over the beaten whites in the bowl, which will rise to the surface, slightly cooked. Dust with mace or grated nutmeg, and serve cold.

Baked Tapioca Pudding.—Butter a quart pudding dish, cover the bottom with tart apples, pared and cored, and pour over them a cup of tapioca that has been soaked for several hours and drained. Add a dust of salt and a cup of boiling water. Sift a tablespoonful of granulated sugar over the top of the pudding, and bake until the tapioca is transparent and the apples are cooked and a light brown color. Serve warm or cold, as preferred, with sugar and cream.

Sea Moss Blanc-Mange.—Wash a small handful of sea moss, Irish moss, or Iceland moss, free from sand and dust. Soak in cold water for half an hour, then put it in a quart of boiling milk, and let steep at boiling heat for twenty or thirty minutes. Test it by putting a spoonful to cool, and if it stiffens like jelly it has steeped long enough. When sufficiently steeped drain off the liquid, and sweeten and flavor to taste. Serve cold, with or without cream.

Baked Custard.—To two cups of rich milk add a pinch of salt and four eggs beaten with four tablespoonfuls of sugar. Stir well together, pour into cups brushed with melted butter, or into a pudding dish, and bake in a pan of water in a slow oven. As soon as the custard becomes stiff in the center it is sufficiently cooked.

Boiled Custard No. 1.—To two cups of boiling milk add a pinch of salt and the yolks of four eggs, beaten very light with one tablespoonful of cold milk. As soon as the egg stiffens pour it into a cold bowl and stir a minute to prevent curdling. Beat the whites of the eggs stiff, add gradually four tablespoonfuls of pulverized sugar and a teaspoonful of vanilla extract. When the custard is cold add the beaten eggs and sugar, whip all well together, and set on ice until ready to serve.

Boiled Custard No. 2.—To three cups of boiling milk add two tablespoonfuls of flour, four tablespoonfuls of granulated sugar, and a pinch of salt, well mixed together. Simmer ten minutes, then add slowly—stirring rapidly meanwhile—the yolks of three eggs beaten light with one tablespoonful of cold milk, and cook to a creamy consistency. Put the beaten whites of the eggs in a china dish and pour the boiling custard over them.

LESSON XII.—A BREAKFAST.

To be prepared by pupils and served to the class under supervision of teacher. Taken principally from dishes prepared and cooked during the second term.

THIRD TERM.

LESSON I.—BROILING, BAKING, AND MIXING.

Arrangement of Lesson.

1. Have two or three pupils each prepare a bird and broil it in the oven.
2. Make pop-overs. Have a small number of pupils make pop-overs at the same time.
3. Have pupils prepare and cook potato balls for creamed potato balls.
4. Have pupils prepare sliced tomatoes, also make a French or mayonnaise dressing for tomato salad.
5. Have pupils broil liver (open fire).
6. Have pupils broil lamb or mutton chops (open fire or gas).
7. Finish creamed potato balls.

Formulas for Lesson I.

To Broil a Bird.—Lay the prepared bird on a towel, flatten with a rolling-pin, put in a wire broiler, place over the fire inside down, and let it remain in that position until well seared, then turn the broiler over, sear the skin side, and so turn and sear alternately until thoroughly broiled. Lift to a warm platter, season, and serve.

Pop-Overs.—One cup of flour, one cup of sweet milk, one egg, and a pinch of salt. Put the egg, flour, salt, and half the milk together in a small bowl, and with a Dover beater whip very light, then gradually add the balance of the milk. Half fill deep gem-pans, and bake forty-five minutes in an oven at the same temperature as for bread.

Creamed Potato Balls.—Cut the potato balls with a vegetable scoop, boil until tender, and serve with a thin white sauce.

To Prepare Tomatoes.—Lay the tomatoes, stem end down, in a basin or bowl, and pour boiling water over them until they are completely covered with it. Let stand half a minute, then drain it off, and fill the bowl with cold water. Renew the water several times, if necessary, but do not handle the tomatoes until quite cold. As soon as the tomatoes are cold the skins can be removed quite easily. Lay them upon ice until just before serving, when the skins can be removed and the tomatoes sliced.

To Broil Liver.—Dust the slices of prepared liver with flour, dip in melted butter, place in the broiler, and broil and serve like beefsteak.

To Broil Chops.—Mutton chops should have most of the fat removed from them and should be trimmed neatly, and broiled and served like beefsteak. A mutton chop should be at least an inch thick.

Lamb chops should be trimmed, broiled, and served like mutton chops. As the fat of lamb is more delicate than the fat of mutton, a larger quantity of fat should be left on a lamb than on a mutton chop. Lamb chops are frequently served on thin slices of dry toast.

LESSON II.—BAKING.

Arrangement of Lesson.

1. Make Boston brown bread (teacher and pupils). An illustration of baking by steam.
2. Make corn-meal mush (pupils).
3. Bake beans. Have beans in various stages of preparation; also the finished product.
4. Bake fish (boned and stuffed).
5. Make corn-meal pudding.
6. Bake tomatoes.
7. Stew salsify.

Formulas for Lesson II.

Boston Brown Bread.—Two cups of corn-meal, two cups of graham flour, one cup of New Orleans molasses, three cups of sour milk or buttermilk, two even teaspoonfuls of soda, two even teaspoonfuls of salt. Mix together the meal, flour, soda, and salt, add the molasses and milk, stir thoroughly, pour into a well-greased mold, cover closely, and steam four or five hours.

To Bake Beans.—Soak a quart of white beans in cold water over night, or for eight or ten hours, then drain and put to cook in sufficient cold water to cover them. Add a teaspoonful of salt and half a teaspoonful of soda, and as soon as the water boils drain it off. Put in the pot in which the beans are to be baked half a pound of salt pork or corned beef and a tablespoonful of white sugar, or twice as much New Orleans molasses. Pour in the beans, fill the pot to within an inch of the top with boiling water, cover with a close-fitting lid, and bake in a very moderate oven from twelve to eighteen hours. As the water evaporates replace it with sufficient boiling water to keep the beans covered during the entire time they are in the oven. If the beans are liked browned they can be poured into a shallow baking pan and put in a hot oven until they are the color desired.

To Bone a Fish.—Cut off its head and insert the point of the boning-knife close to the back-bone, under the small bones that lie near the inside surface of the fish. Slip the knife under these bones and carefully lift them from the fish, leaving the meat as little disturbed or broken as possible. With a round-pointed, dull-bladed knife scrape the flesh away from the back-bone and the bones that project into the fish therefrom, until they can be lifted away clear of the flesh ; then with the blade of the knife smooth and pack together the flesh that has been disturbed by removing them. It is not advisable to bone small fish, and all fish, as well as meats of every kind, are of finer flavor when cooked with the bones in them.

Stuffing for Fish.—Enrich with butter one pint of soft bread crumbs, season with pepper, salt, and one tablespoonful of minced onion sautéd in butter. Fill the fish with stuffing and sew it up. Put slices of pork or breakfast bacon in the baking pan, and lay the fish on them. Cover the upper side in a similar manner with slices of pork or bacon, then set in the oven, and close the door until the fish is cooked. If the oven is at the proper temperature the fish will require no attention. A medium-sized fish will bake in three quarters of an hour.

Baked Corn-meal Pudding.—To one cup of well-boiled corn-meal mush add one teaspoonful of butter, and one teaspoonful of ginger mixed with two tablespoonfuls of granulated sugar. Stir in gradually one cup of sweet milk, then add two well-beaten eggs. Bake in a buttered pudding dish until it is firm in the center and remove from the oven before it is wheyed. Serve warm, with sweet cream.

Baked Tomatoes.—Wash and wipe medium-sized tomatoes, cut them in halves, and place, skin side down, in a baking dish. Then season with salt, pepper, and sugar, if liked, cover with buttered bread crumbs, and bake until the crumbs are nicely browned and the tomatoes well cooked.

To Stew Salsify.—Pare, cut in pieces half an inch in length, stew half an hour, or till tender, drain, and serve with drawn butter or white sauce; or mash fine, when drained, season with salt and pepper, add a little cream, and serve. Salsify should be laid in cold water as soon as pared, to keep it from becoming discolored. When food material becomes discolored from exposure to the atmosphere, such exposure injures its flavor perceptibly. Therefore great care should be observed to preserve the natural color of all food materials.

LESSON III.—BOILING.

Arrangement of Lesson.

1. Have pupils make lamb fricassee.
2. Steam fish.
3. Have pupils steam rice.
4. Have pupils steam potatoes.
5. Boil eggs, soft and hard.
6. Poach eggs (on toast).
7. Have pupils make caramel blanc-mange. Caramel custard. (Test of proficiency.)
8. Have pupils make drawn butter sauce for the fish. (Test.)

Formulas for Lesson III.

Fricasseeing.—Stews are often, but incorrectly, termed fricassees. A fricassee is a combination of a sauté and a stew, and the meat for a fricassee should always be sautéd or browned before it is put to stew. This sautéing or browning is best done in a small quantity of clarified butter, although drippings of beef or veal may be used, if preferred.

To Fricassee Lamb.—Prepare the lamb as for stewing. Season the pieces with salt and pepper, roll in flour, fry or sauté until light brown in color, then place in the stewing kettle. Put a pint of water in the pan in which the lamb was browned and after it has simmered five minutes pour it over the lamb. Cover the kettle closely and let the lamb simmer gently until cooked. Lift into a platter when done, and if there is not sufficient sauce add more water, and more flour, if required, to that in the kettle, cook five minutes, and strain over the lamb.

To Steam a Fish.—Dust a prepared fish, inside and outside, with salt. Dredge the outside lightly with flour, wrap in a cloth, and place in a steamer over boiling water. Cover the steamer closely, and cook until the fish will flake easily. A five-pound fish will steam in half an hour. Serve on a hot platter in a napkin. Serve with it, in a tureen, drawn butter, parsley sauce, egg sauce, or sauce hollandaise.

To Steam Rice.—Pick over and wash the rice. Put it in the dish in which it is to be served and add a level teaspoonful of salt and three cups of boiling water to each cup of rice. Set in a steamer over boiling water, and cook half an hour, or until the rice is tender. Milk may be mixed with the water in any proportion desired; or, if preferred, milk alone may be used instead of water.

To Steam Potatoes.—Place the potatoes, either pared or unpared, in a steamer over boiling water. Cover closely and cook forty-five minutes, or until the potatoes are done, which can be ascertained by testing them with a fork. Serve in a napkin in a heated dish, and fold the corners of the napkin over the potatoes.

Sweet potatoes can be steamed in the same manner.

To Boil Eggs.—See Lesson IV., Term I.

To Poach an Egg.—Break the egg into a cup, from which slip it carefully into water at boiling temperature, but not actively boiling. Let it remain until cooked as desired, then lift from the water with a spatula or skimmer, and serve on dipped or buttered toast. The water in which eggs are poached should be well salted.

LESSON IV.—BOILING AND MIXING.

Arrangement of Lesson.

1. Braise beef with spices and vegetables.
2. Make brown soups. (Teacher and pupils.)
3. Have pupils make plain batter puddings and steam them.
4. Make fish chowder.
5. Have pupils prepare and cook asparagus.
6. Have pupils prepare and cook spinach.
7. Have pupils make strawberry and vanilla sauces for puddings.

Formulas for Lesson IV.

Braising.—Braising, like fricasseeing, is a combination of frying or sautéing and stewing. It is usually done, however, in an oven, in a braising pan having a close-fitting cover. The advantages of braising over stewing, for certain articles, are that a more uniform temperature can be obtained and the flavors of the food be better preserved on account of there being less evaporation. Braising is an excellent mode of cooking tough meats and poultry.

To Braise Beef.—An aitchbone, or a piece from the upper part of the round, is a good cut for braising. Season lightly with salt and pepper, roll in flour, brown in clarified butter or drippings, in a frying pan or spider, then put in a braising kettle with an onion, a carrot, a turnip, and three cloves. Add half as much water as for stewing, cover closely, set in a moderate oven, and let cook slowly for several hours.

Mixed Stock.—Take the trimmings of beef, veal, mutton, lamb, or meat of any kind, the shank bone of a ham, the roots and trimmings of celery, the odds and ends of corn, beans, or peas, and an onion, a turnip, and a carrot. Skin, wash, or otherwise prepare them. Put them altogether into a stock pot—putting the bones in first—add salt, six or eight cloves, and a small pepper pod, if at hand, and cover with cold water. Set to cook, let simmer five hours, strain into a bowl, and let cool. When cool remove the grease and the stock will be ready for use.

Brown Soup No. 1.—Cook together in a sauce-pan, until brown, one tablespoonful of butter and two tablespoonfuls of flour. Add four cups of soup stock, simmer five minutes, season to taste, and serve.

Brown Soup No. 2.—Cook together in a sauce-pan, until brown, one tablespoonful of butter and two tablespoonfuls of flour. Add four cups of any kind of stock, one cup of strained tomato, one teaspoonful of sugar, and half a teaspoonful of curry powder. Simmer ten minutes, season to taste, and serve.

Steamed Pudding.—Sift together two teaspoonfuls of baking powder, half a teaspoonful of salt, and two cups of flour. Rub into it two tablespoonfuls of butter. Add a cup of milk, make a dough soft enough to drop from the spoon. Fill a buttered pudding mold three fourths full of the dough and steam an hour and a half.

Fish Chowder.—Prepare four cups of fresh codfish by removing the skin and bones and cutting the fish in pieces about an inch square. Cut a quarter of a pound of salt pork into thin slices. Divide the slices into strips and sauté in a spider until brown and crisp. Put the browned pork into a sauce-pan and add to it a minced onion and a tablespoonful of butter. Pare and cut in dice a quart of potatoes. Break into pieces three or four pilot biscuit. To the pork and onion add the fish, potato, and biscuit in alternate layers. Season to taste with salt and pepper. Cover with hot water. Put a tight-fitting lid on the sauce-pan, and simmer gently for half an hour, or until the potato is cooked. Add two cups of hot cream or milk, and serve.

To Boil Asparagus.—Wash the asparagus, tie it in small bundles, cook till tender, and serve on toast, with melted butter, white sauce, or sauce hollandaise.

To Boil Spinach.—Put the prepared spinach in a small quantity of boiling water, cover closely, boil ten minutes, or till tender, drain in a colander, press out the water, season with salt, pepper, and butter.

Strawberry Sauce.—Mix a tablespoonful of flour with a cup of granulated sugar, add a cup of hot water, simmer five minutes, remove from the fire, and stir into the mixture a cup of crushed strawberries and half a cup of creamed butter.

Vanilla Sauce.—See Liquid Sauce.

LESSON V.—MIXING AND FRYING.

ARRANGEMENT OF LESSON.

1. Make nun's puffs.
2. Have pupils make doughnuts with eggs and sweet milk.
3. Have pupils make doughnuts with sour milk and soda.
4. Have pupils make plain fritters.
5. Have pupils make apple fritters.
6. Fry nun's puffs.
7. Fry corn-meal mush.

FORMULAS FOR LESSON V.

Nun's Puffs.—Put a cupful of water in a sauce-pan over the fire, add half a cupful, light measure, of butter, and when it boils stir in three fourths of a cupful of flour, and cook five minutes, stirring constantly with a wooden spoon. Remove from the fire, and when cool, not cold, stir in, one by one, four eggs. Drop, a teaspoonful at a time, into hot grease, being careful not to get the frying kettle too full, as the puffs enlarge very much while cooking. Let them remain in the kettle about five minutes, drain carefully on cheese-cloth, and when cold dust with cinnamon and pulverized sugar. Or omit the cinnamon and sugar, make an incision in each puff, and fill with whipped cream flavored with vanilla and sweetened.

Fried Doughnuts.—Sift three pints of flour into a mixing bowl. Make a well in the center, into which put half a pint of sugar, a quarter of a pint of sour milk, two eggs, two tablespoonfuls of butter, a teaspoonful of soda, and an eighth of a nutmeg, grated. Mix these ingredients well together, and work in the flour gradually until a dough is formed sufficiently stiff to be rolled upon a well-floured board into a sheet half an inch in thickness. Cut in any shape desired, fry in hot grease, and drain on cheese-cloth. When cold dust with pulverized sugar. Sweet milk and a heaping teaspoonful of baking powder can be used in place of sour milk and soda.

Plain Fritters.—Stir together a pint of flour, half a pint of cold water, the yolks of four eggs, two tablespoonfuls of sugar, two tablespoonfuls of olive oil or melted butter, and half a teaspoonful of salt. Beat with a Dover beater until very light, then mix in the whites of the eggs beaten stiff, and fry in hot grease, dropping in a tablespoonful at a time. Drain on cheese-cloth, dust with pulverized sugar, and serve.

Apple Fritters.—Select smooth, medium-sized, sour apples. Pare whole, remove the cores, slice in rounds an eighth of an inch in thickness, dip in batter prepared as for plain fritters, fry in hot grease until a nice brown, drain on cheese-cloth, dust with pulverized sugar, and serve.

Fried Mush.—Cut cold mush into squares, cubes, or oblong pieces a suitable size for serving, cover with flour and meal sifted together, dip in egg batter, roll in crumbs, fry in a basket in hot fat, until a rich brown color, drain on cheese-cloth, and serve in a napkin ; or use to garnish broiled or fried chicken or fish.

LESSON VI.—MIXING.

ARRANGEMENT OF LESSON.

1. Scallop eggs.
2. Scramble eggs.
3. Shirr eggs.
4. Make creamy omelet.
5. Have pupils make creamy omelet.
6. Make omelet soufflé.
7. Have pupils make omelet soufflé.

FORMULAS FOR LESSON VI.

Scalloped Eggs.—Slice or dice cold boiled eggs, put them in a buttered baking dish, cover with white sauce, and heat to boiling point in a moderate oven.

Scrambled Eggs.—Put in an omelet pan half a teaspoonful of butter for each egg. When the butter is hot pour in the eggs, without beating, and when set on the bottom of the pan mix or scramble them lightly with a fork or spoon. Cook as desired, season to taste, and serve. Minced parsley is an excellent flavoring for scrambled eggs.

Shirred Eggs.—Put in a shirred egg dish a teaspoonful of melted butter for each egg. Break the eggs separately, slip carefully into the dish, bake to taste in a moderate oven, season with salt and pepper, and serve.

Creamy Omelet.—Beat together lightly four eggs and four teaspoonfuls of water, milk, or cream, just enough to break and mix sufficient to allow a spoonful of the mixture to be dipped up. Heat, but be careful not to brown, a tablespoonful of butter in an omelet pan. Have a pan that will correspond in size to the number of eggs used, so that the beaten mixture will cover the bottom to the depth of at least half an inch. Pour in the mixture and place the pan over a quick heat, add salt and pepper to taste, and as soon as the egg "sets" or stiffens slightly upon the bottom of the pan lift it up lightly and carefully with a fork, so the uncooked egg can take the place of that which is cooked. Continue this lifting process as long as there is any uncooked egg in the pan, and until all the mixture lies in a soft creamy pile of a delicate golden hue. Permit the bottom to set quite firmly, then tip the pan slightly, loosen the edges with a broad-bladed, limber knife, or spatula, slip it under one side of the omelet, and fold over, tipping the pan at the same time to facilitate the folding. Then, by still further tipping the pan, turn the omelet, nicely folded, on a platter and serve hot.

Omelet Souffle.—To the well-beaten yolks of two eggs add three teaspoonfuls of sugar, one teaspoonful of lemon juice, and half a teaspoonful of lemon, orange, vanilla, or any flavoring extract liked. Beat very light and fold in the whites of four eggs beaten stiff. Put in a hot omelet pan, well greased, and cook ten or twelve minutes, in a very moderate oven. Slip on to a warm dish, without folding. A pinch of cream of tartar added to the whites of the eggs improves all omelets containing no other acid.

LESSON VII.—MIXING.

Suet and Egg Pastry.

ARRANGEMENT OF LESSON.

1. Make suet pastry.
2. Have pupils make suet pastry.
3. Make meat pie.
4. Make suet pudding.
5. Make egg pastry.
6. Have pupils make egg pastry into strudels and noodles.
7. Rewarm cold meats in sauces.
8. Make hash.
9. Have a number of pupils use suet pastry for meat pies; others use suet pastry for dumplings. Steam in cups and cloths.

FORMULAS FOR LESSON VII.

Suet Pastry.—To three cups of flour add one cup of finely shredded beef suet, three teaspoonfuls of baking powder, and one teaspoonful of salt. Mix, with cold water, or cold sweet milk, to a soft dough.

Beefsteak Pie.—Line the sides of a pudding dish with suet pastry, and fill three fourths full with uncooked beefsteak, diced, minced, or hashed, and seasoned to taste. With every cup of prepared meat mix a level teaspoonful of flour, cover with a crust, and bake until the pie is cooked.

Suet Pudding.—Prepare like suet pastry, and mold with the tips of the fingers into an oval-shaped loaf, about three times as long as wide. Wring a napkin from hot water, dust with flour, lay the loaf upon it, fold the napkin up over the loaf, place in a steamer, and cook an hour and a half. Serve with liquid sauce from which the butter has been omitted.

Egg Pastry.—To one egg, slightly beaten, add a pinch of salt, a tablespoonful of melted butter, and flour sufficient to make a soft dough. Knead in the flour with the finger-tips until the dough is smooth and very elastic, and can be kneaded without flour and without sticking to the molding board. When properly made, egg paste can be rolled as thin as a sheet of paper.

Apple Strudels.—Roll out a piece of egg pastry until it is large enough to cover a pie-pan, but only half as thick as flaky pie crust. Cover it nearly to the edge with sour apples sliced very thin and seasoned to taste with sugar and ground cinnamon. Roll up like a roly-poly, pinch the edges securely together, lay upon a greased pan, and bake half an hour, or until cooked. Serve warm.

Noodles.—Roll egg pastry very thin, dust lightly with flour, roll up, and cut in shreds. Boil in salted water twenty minutes.

Creamed Meats.—To one cup of white sauce seasoned with celery, parsley, or onion, add two cups of cold turkey, chicken, veal, or fish, freed from skin and bones and cut in dice. Cook until thoroughly heated.

Meats Rewarmed in Brown Sauce.—To two thirds of a cup of brown sauce add one third of a cup of strained tomato, season to taste with salt and pepper, and add to it two cups of cold meat (beef, mutton, lamb, or other dark meat preferred), cut in dice. Simmer five minutes and serve.

Breakfast Hash.—To one cup of coarsely hashed cold boiled or baked potato add one cup of finely hashed cold meat, either beef, veal, lamb, chicken, or a mixture of any or all of them, season to taste with salt and pepper, add two or three tablespoonfuls of broth, gravy, milk, or cream, and brown in a buttered pan on the range, or in the oven. Or heat thoroughly, without browning, if preferred.

LESSON VIII.—MIXING.

Croquettes.

ARRANGEMENT OF LESSON.

1. Make Chicken or Veal Croquettes No. 1.
2. Make Chicken or Veal Croquettes No. 2.
3. Make potato croquettes.
4. Cook rice croquettes.
5. Have pupils make French toast.
6. Have pupils make tropical toast.
7. Have pupils make Japanese fritters.
8. Sauté bananas.
9. Bake bananas.

Have each pupil make croquettes.

FORMULAS FOR LESSON VIII.

Chicken Croquettes No. 1.—To one cup of finely

chopped chicken, either boiled, stewed, or roasted, add half a cup of bread crumbs, softened in half a cup of sweet cream, one teaspoonful of melted butter, salt and pepper to taste, and the unbeaten white of an egg. Mix-well together, fry in spoonfuls in hot fat, drain on cheese-cloth, and serve in a napkin, garnished with lemon points and curled parsley.

Chicken Croquettes No. 2.—To half a cup of white sauce, made by cooking together one tablespoonful of butter and one of flour with half a cup of sweet cream, add a cup of cooked chicken, finely hashed, a teaspoonful of minced onion, half a teaspoonful of minced parsley, and salt and pepper to taste. Spread on a greased plate to cool, and when cold form into croquettes, cover with egg batter, roll in crumbs, fry in a basket in hot fat, and drain on cheese-cloth.

Potato Croquettes.—Peel and boil one medium-sized onion and three potatoes. Drain, dry off, mash fine, add a tablespoonful of rich cream and a teaspoonful of butter, or a tablespoonful each of butter and milk—an additional spoonful of milk may be added if necessary to make the mixture sufficiently soft—season with salt and pepper, and beat with a wooden spoon till light. When slightly stiffened by cooling, shape into any form desired by rolling lightly under the hand on a smooth board, cover with crumbs, then with egg batter, then again with crumbs, and fry in deep fat.

Rice Croquettes.—To a cupful of boiled rice add half a cupful of sweet milk, a tablespoonful of sugar, and a teaspoonful of butter. Put in a sauce-pan over the fire and simmer gently, stirring frequently, until the rice has absorbed the milk. Remove and, when slightly cooled, flavor with half a teaspoonful of lemon extract, add the white of an egg, unbeaten, fry in hot grease, dropping in a spoonful at a time, drain on cheese-cloth, and serve with pulverized sugar or with fruit sauce.

French Toast.—Beat one egg very light, gradually beat into it a cup of sweet milk, and add a generous pinch of salt. Remove the crust from half a dozen slices of bread about a quarter of an inch thick, lay them upon a platter, and pour part of the egg and milk mixture over them. After they have soaked a minute turn them over carefully, add the balance of the mixture, and after they have soaked another minute drain and sauté in clarified butter until richly browned. Serve hot with a liquid sauce, in place of a pudding, or serve at breakfast, without sauce.

Tropical Toast.—Prepare and cook the slices of bread as for French toast. To one cup of well-cooked raisins add half a cup of flaked pine-apple, and half a cup of orange pulp cut in small pieces. Sweeten to taste. Heat all together and serve a spoonful of fruit on each slice of toast. Or the pine-apple may be omitted, and half a cup of thinly sliced bananas used in its place.

Japanese Fritters.—Cut slices of bread one inch thick, one inch wide, and four inches long. Prepare as for French toast, roll in dried bread crumbs, and fry in deep fat. Serve with a fruit sauce.

To Saute Bananas.—Peel the bananas, split them in halves lengthwise, dust with sugar, roll in melted butter, and cook till brown in a spider over the fire, or in a roasting pan in a hot oven.

To Bake Bananas.—Peel the bananas, roll in melted butter and granulated sugar, lay a little distance apart in a roasting pan, and brown in a hot oven. Shake the pan occasionally while the bananas are baking.

LESSON IX.—MIXING.

Sponge Cake Mixtures.[1]

ARRANGEMENT OF LESSON.

1. Make sponge cake. (Teacher and pupils working together.)
2. Make angel cake. (Teacher and pupils.)
3. Make sunshine cake. (Teacher and pupils.)

FORMULAS FOR LESSON IX.

Sponge Cake.—Ten eggs, their weight in fine granulated sugar, half their weight in flour, juice and grated rind of a lemon. Break the eggs, separate the whites from the yolks, and reject two of the yolks. Put the eight yolks, with the lemon juice and grated peel, into a bowl and whip very light with a Dover beater, then beat in gradually two thirds of the sugar. Beat the whites of the eggs stiff, and whip into them the remaining third of the sugar. Add the yolks to the whites, folding in carefully, then add the flour, sifting it in a little at a time, and mixing it carefully, by folding rather than by beating. Bake in a moderate oven from

[1] See "The Art of Cookery" for further information on cake-making.

twenty minutes to an hour, according to the depth of the pans.

Angel Cake.—One cup of white of egg, one heaping cup of winter wheat flour, one and a half cups of fine granulated sugar, one level teaspoonful of cream of tartar, one teaspoonful of almond extract. Eggs vary so much in size that it is better to take a certain measure of the white than a certain number of the eggs. Put the measured whites in an earthen bowl, break lightly with an egg whip, sift in the cream of tartar, and beat until the egg will cling to the bowl and not slip out if the bowl is turned upside down, then beat the sugar into the egg, sifting it in gradually, add the flavoring, and lastly sift in the flour, stirring only enough to combine it with the egg and sugar. Put the mixture in an ungreased pan, the bottom of which has been covered with white paper, place carefully in an oven of moderate temperature, and cover with a baking sheet or tin, so as to protect the top of the cake but not exclude the air. Remove the cover in half an hour—when the cake should be perfectly risen—and bake half an hour longer. When taken from the oven turn the pan bottom upwards, and if it has no center tube rest it upon cups or bowls until the cake is perfectly cold, then remove by slipping a thin-bladed knife between the cake and the sides of the pan. Success in making angel cake depends largely upon having an oven of the proper temperature. If the oven is too warm the cake will be tough.

Sunshine Cake.—Yolks of the eggs used for the

angel cake and one whole egg, one cup of water, one and one half cups of fine granulated sugar, three cups of flour, three teaspoonfuls of baking powder, one teaspoonful of vanilla, one of orange extract, three tablespoonfuls of melted butter. Beat the eggs, adding the sugar gradually, until very light. Add the water with the flavoring, and the flour with the baking powder alternately. Stir in the melted butter. Beat well and bake at a slightly greater heat than is required for angel cake.

LESSON X.—MIXING.

Gelatine Jellies.

ARRANGEMENT OF LESSON.

1. Lemon jelly.
2. Orange jelly.
3. Snow pudding.
4. Charlotte russe.
5. Coffee cream.
6. Custard for snow pudding.

    Apportion the work, and let each pupil put to soak the amount of gelatine necessary, at the beginning of the lesson.

Give instruction in the use of gelatine.

FORMULAS FOR LESSON X.

Lemon Jelly.—To one third of a box of gelatine add one cup of cold water, soak an hour, add a cup of hot water, half a cup of lemon juice, a teaspoonful of lemon extract, and two cups of granulated sugar. Stir until the sugar is dissolved, then set on ice until jellied and ready to serve.

When phosphated or acidulated gelatine is used in making lemon jelly or snow pudding omit the juice of one lemon ; when it is used in making jellies, puddings, creams, etc., of other fruits omit the lemon juice entirely.

Orange Jelly.—To one third of a box of gelatine add one cup of cold water, let soak an hour, add half a cup of boiling water, one cup of granulated sugar, one cup of orange juice, the juice of one lemon, and a teaspoonful of orange extract. Stir until the sugar is dissolved, then set on ice until jellied and ready to serve.

Snow Pudding.—Prepare lemon jelly as directed, and when it begins to jelly and is slightly thickened all through, whip with a Dover beater until perfectly light, then add the whites of three eggs beaten stiff, to which has been added a pinch of salt and three tablespoonfuls of granulated sugar. Whip all well together, and set on ice until firm. Serve with a boiled custard.

Charlotte Russe.—To one fourth of a box of gelatine add half a cup of cold water and soak an hour, then add half a cup of hot milk and a tablespoonful of granulated sugar. Stir until the sugar is dissolved, strain into a two-quart bowl, surrounded with ice and water, and add a cup of cold cream and a teaspoonful of vanilla extract. When the liquid begins to jelly beat vigorously with a Dover egg-beater until it is very light, then add the whites of two eggs beaten light, to which has been added a pinch of salt and two tablespoonfuls of granulated sugar. Remove the beater, and, with a strong whip or a wooden spoon, beat into the mixture a pint of whipped cream. Pour into molds, and set on ice till ready to serve.

Coffee Cream.—Add to one third of a box of soaked gelatine one and one half cups of strong hot coffee. Stir until dissolved, add one cup of white sugar made into caramel. When cool and beginning to jelly, whip with a Dover egg-beater until light. Add two cups of whipped cream, and put in a cold place till served.

Boiled Custard.—To two cups of boiling milk add a pinch of salt and the yolks of three eggs, beaten very light with one tablespoonful of cold milk. As soon as the egg stiffens pour it into a cold bowl, and stir a minute to prevent curdling.

LESSON XI.—ICE CREAM AND ICES.[1]

ARRANGEMENT OF LESSON.

1. Lemon ice.
2. Orange ice.
3. Ice Cream No. 1.
4. Ice Cream No. 2.
5. Mousse.

Work divided among pupils, directed by teacher.

FORMULAS FOR LESSON XI.

Lemon Ice.—To four cups of boiling water add two

[1] "Principles of Artificial Freezing," Youmans's "Handbook of Household Science."

cups of sugar, boil five minutes, remove from the fire, add half a cup of lemon juice and a teaspoonful and a half of lemon extract. Strain, pour into a freezer, and freeze.

Orange Ice.—To two cups of boiling water add a cup and a half of granulated sugar, boil five minutes, remove from the fire, add two cups of orange juice, the juice of a lemon, and a teaspoonful and a half of orange extract. Strain, pour into a freezer, and freeze.

Ice Cream No. 1.—To one quart of thin cream add three quarters of a cup of granulated sugar and one tablespoonful of vanilla extract. Strain and freeze.

Ice Cream No. 2.—To one pint of boiling milk add three quarters of a cup of granulated sugar and one tablespoonful of flour, sifted together. Cook five minutes, add a pint of thin cream, let boil, and remove from the fire. When cold flavor to taste with vanilla or lemon extract, add the unbeaten whites of two eggs, and freeze.

Mousse.—Flavor one pint of rich cream with one teaspoonful of vanilla and one half cup of sugar made into caramel. When very cold whip, put into a mold, pack in ice, and let stand from one to three hours.

LESSON XII.—A DINNER.

Prepared and served by class to six guests.

APPENDIX.

APPENDIX.

I.

Individual Proportions.

The following formulas from Lessons VIII., IX., X. of the first term have been prepared as an illustration of the manner of reducing them for individual practice in the classroom. These formulas have simply been divided by four, and in a similar manner most of the formulas can be easily divided when desirable.

LESSON VIII.

Wheat Muffins No. 1.—One half cup of flour, one fourth cup of sweet milk, one teaspoonful of melted butter, one teaspoonful of baking powder, one half salt-spoonful of salt.

Wheat Muffins No. 2.—Three fourths cup of flour, one half cup of thick sour milk, one fourth teaspoonful of soda, one half salt-spoonful of salt.

Griddle Cakes.—One half cup of flour, one third cup of sweet milk, one half teaspoonful of baking powder, one teaspoonful of melted butter, one third of an egg, salt.

LESSON IX.

Baking Powder Biscuit.—One half cup of flour,

one fourth cup of sweet milk, one half teaspoonful of baking powder, one half salt-spoonful of salt.

Corn Muffins.—One half cup of granulated corn-meal, three eighths cup of boiling water, one fourth cup of cold sweet milk, one teaspoonful of sugar, one half teaspoonful of salt, half an egg.

LESSON IX.

Corn-bread.—One half cup of corn-meal, five eighths cup of boiling milk, one half teaspoonful of butter, one teaspoonful of sugar, one half teaspoonful of salt, one egg.

LESSON X.

Vegetable Soup.—One half cup of beef stock, one tablespoonful of carrot, one tablespoonful of turnip, one tablespoonful of onion, one tablespoonful of tomato, one salt-spoonful of minced parsley.

Bread and Butter Pudding No. 1.—Butter one slice of stale bread thinly on both sides, and cover the bottom of a shallow dish. Pour as much sweet milk over the bread as it will absorb, then pour over it a custard made from two thirds of a cup of milk, one fourth salt-spoonful of salt, and one well-beaten egg. Bake, and serve hot with creamed butter and sugar.

Bread and Butter Pudding No. 2.—Prepare the same as No. 1, adding one tablespoonful of sugar to the custard. Dust with nutmeg and serve cold.

Bread and Butter Pudding No. 3.—Prepare the same as No. 1, but add to the custard two tablespoonfuls of caramel.

II.

Utensils Required for Twelve Pupils in a Classroom.

CHINA-WARE.—1 dozen custard cups; 1 dozen half-pint bowls; 1 dozen pint bowls; 1 dozen quart bowls; 1 dozen two-quart bowls; 6 three-quart bowls; 2 four-quart bowls; 12 plates, small size; 12 plates, large size; 12 cups and saucers; 1 set of platters; 5 small vegetable dishes; 6 larger vegetable dishes; 2 two-quart pitchers; 2 quart pitchers; 2 pint pitchers; 12 shirred egg dishes.

GRANITE-WARE.—12 double boilers, one quart; 12 quart sauce-pans; 6 three-pint sauce-pans; 6 two-quart sauce-pans; 12 stew-pans, one quart; 1 three-quart kettle; 1 four-quart kettle; 12 pie-pans, smallest size; 6 pie-pans, largest size; 1 roasting pan, 14x10 inches; 2 roasting pans, smaller size; 1 fish-pan; 2 basting spoons; 6 omelet pans; 1 tea kettle; 1 griddle spade; 1 colander; 1 coffee pot; 1 tea pot; 1 pitcher, three pints.

WOODEN-WARE.—6 rolling-pins; 4 wooden spoons, various sizes; 1 potato masher; 1 chopping tray; 1 tray for knife cleaning; 3 meat boards; 1 bread board; 1 potato slicer; 2 pastry brushes; 1 nest of boxes; 1 nest of buckets.

GLASS.—1 dozen quart fruit jars; 1 dozen pint fruit jars; 6 lemon reamers.

LINEN.—Dish towels; dish cloths; hand towels; holders; cheese-cloth.

STEELWARE.—1 carving knife and fork; 1 bread knife; 1 vegetable scoop; 1 large boning knife; 1 medium boning knife; 1 steel knife-sharpener; scales; skewers; 1 can opener; 1 cork screw; 1 set of Christy knives.

IRONWARE.—1 deep Scotch frying kettle; 3 griddles, various sizes; 2 wire baskets for frying; 3 toasting forks.

TINWARE.—2 wire broilers; 1 oyster broiler; small scoops; spice boxes and tray; 12 small bread-pans, 4x3 inches; 12 small cake-pans, round; 6 brick loaf bread-pans; pans for soup sticks; pans for finger rolls; pans for long French rolls; 6 gingerbread or biscuit pans; 3 sets of muffin pans; 3 sets of gem-pans, square; 12 patty pans; 6 biscuit cutters; 6 doughnut cutters; 1 squash strainer; 1 soup strainer; 1 sink strainer; dish-pans; 1 ice cream freezer; 1 ice shovel; 1 ice pick, shaver; 1 meat cutter; 1 wire potato masher; 1 steam cooker; 1 large-mouthed funnel; 2 smaller funnels; 2 flour sieves; 1 grater, medium size; 2 smaller graters; 1 whip churn; 1 lemon squeezer; 2 egg poachers.

EACH MEMBER OF THE CLASS REQUIRES.—2 measuring cups, one divided into quarters, the other divided into thirds; 1 flour dredge; 1 salt dredge; 1 pepper dredge; 1 knife and fork; 1 paring knife; 2 wooden spoons, one small size and one larger; 1 Daisy egg-beater; 1 Dover egg-beater, small; 1 fine strainer or sifter; 1 tablespoon; 1 teaspoon; 1 salt-spoon; 1 palette knife, medium size; square oil cloth, 12x12 inches; 1 vegetable brush; 1 molding board; if pupils wash the dishes, 1 dish-pan.

III.

Reference Books for Teachers.

Mrs. E. P. Ewing: "The Art of Cookery."
Mathieu Williams: "Chemistry of Cookery."
Sir Henry Thompson: "Food and Feeding."
Sir Henry Thompson: "Diet in Health and Disease."
I. Burney Yeo: "Food in Health and Disease."
Prof. W. O. Atwater: "Chemistry and Economy of Food."
U. S. Department of Agriculture: Bulletin No. 21.
Atwater: "Foods: Nutritive Value and Cost." Bulletin No. 23.
Atwater: "Food and Diet."
Chas. D. Woods: "Meats: Composition and Cooking." Bulletin No. 34.
The University of Chicago: "Our Food, Its Composition and Nutritive Value." Syllabus No. 89.
Edward Atkinson: "Science of Nutrition."
Youmans: "Handbook of Household Science."
Johnston: "Chemistry of Common Life."
Dr. Mary H. Green: "Food Products of the World."
Goodfellow: "Dietetic Value of Bread."
Jago: "Chemistry of Wheat Flour and Bread."
Mrs. Helen Campbell: "Household Economics."
Goodholm: "Domestic Cyclopedia."
Mrs. Ellen H. Richards: "Chemistry of Cooking and Cleaning."

T. Mitchell Prudden, M.D.: "Dust and its Dangers."
Prudden: "Story of the Bacteria."
Theodore Child: "Delicate Feasting."
Schutzenberger: "Fermentation."

INDEX TO FORMULAS.

Apple strudels	113
Apples, to bake, No. 1	34
" " No. 2	34
" to sauté	81
" to stew	40
Asparagus, to boil	107
Bacon, to sauté	44
Baking powder biscuit	60
Bananas, to bake	117
" to sauté	116
Beans, to bake	100
Beef, to braise	105
" to prepare a roast of	33
" to roast	33
Bird, to boil a	98
" to draw a	70
Blanc-mange, cornstarch	94
" " farina	94
" " sea moss	96
Boston brown bread	100
Braising	105
Bread, compressed yeast	52
" liquid yeast	55
" to toast	31
Bread-making	45
Breakfast, a	97
Buns	89
Butter and sugar, creamed	66
Cabbage, to boil	37
Cake, angel	118
" coffee	88
" plain cup	91
" soft ginger	90
" sponge	117
" sunshine	118
Calf's liver, to sauté	44
Carrots, to boil	37
Cereals, to cook	39
Charlotte russe	121
Cheese straws	87
Chicken gravy	76
" scalloped	83
" to boil a	71
" to roast a	74
Chops, to broil	99
Clarified butter	43
Codfish balls	80
Coffee, to make	41
Cookies, plain sugar	91
Corn-bread	63
Corn-meal	61
Cranberries, to stew	75
Cream, coffee	120
Crescents	58
Croquettes, chicken, No. 1	114
" " No. 2	115
" potato	115
" rice	115
Crumbs for frying	44
" to prepare	93

Index to Formulas.

Cucumbers, to prepare	93
Custard, baked	96
" boiled	120
" " No. 1	96
" " No. 2	96
Dinner, a	122
Doughnuts, fried	108
Drawn butter	38
Dressing, cream	67
" French	92
" mayonnaise	67, 92
Dumplings	79
Eggs, scalloped	110
" scrambled	110
" shirred	110
" to boil	36
" to poach	104
Fish cakes, to sauté	81
" chowder	107
" to bone a	101
" to broil a	72
" to fry	43
" to steam a	104
Flour	47
Fowl, to boil a	77
" to draw a	70
" to pick a	69
" to wash a	71
Fricasseeing	103
Fritters, apple	109
" Japanese	116
" plain	109
Graham bread	89
Gravy, chicken	76
" for roast pork	76

Gravy, plain	41
" roast beef	34
Griddle cakes, corn	63
" " wheat, No. 1	59
" " " No. 2	60
Hash	114
Ice cream No. 1	122
" " No. 2	122
" lemon	121
" orange	122
Jelly, lemon	119
" orange	120
Lamb, to boil a leg of	36
" to fricassee	103
" to prepare a leg of	35
Lettuce, to prepare	93
Liver, to broil	99
Luncheon, a	68
Macaroni, scalloped	84
" to boil	39
Meats, creamed	113
" rewarmed	113
Mousse	122
Muffins, corn	63
" wheat, No. 1	59
" " No. 2	59
Mush, corn-meal	40
" fried	109
Mutton broth	38
" to boil a leg of	36
" to prepare a leg of	35
Noodles	113

Index to Formulas. 133

Omelet, creamy	110
" soufflé	111
Onions, to stew	77
Oysters, scalloped	84
" to boil	73
" to fry	81
" to sauté	82
Parsley butter	73
Pastry, egg	113
" suet	112
Pie, apple	86
" beefsteak	112
" crust, flaky	85
" custard	86
" lemon	86
" scrap meat	61
Pop-overs	99
Pork, to roast	75
Potato balls, creamed	99
" lyonnaise	82
" salad	68
Potatoes, browned sweet	76
" browned white	76
" scalloped, No. 1	83
" " No. 2	83
" to bake	34
" to boil	37
" to fry	42
" to prepare	33
" to sauté	81
" to steam	104
Pudding, baked apple	65
" baked corn-meal	102
" baked tapioca	95
" bread and butter, No. 1	64
" bread and butter, No. 2	65

Pudding, bread and butter, No. 3	65
" graham	77
" snow	120
" steamed	106
" suet	112
Puffs, nun's	108
Raisins, to clean	77
Rice, to boil	37
" to steam	104
" to wash	37
Rolls, cinnamon	88
" French, No. 1	57
" " No. 2	57
" " No. 3	57
" imperial	56
" Queen Ann	58
Sago, creamed	95
Salad, cabbage	67
" chicken	93
" fish	93
" lettuce and cucumber	93
" onion	67
" potato	68
Salsify, to stew	102
Sauce, brown	41
" caramel	64
" celery	78
" drawn butter	78
" hollandaise	66
" liquid	65
" oyster	78
" parsley	78
" strawberry	107
" vanilla	107
" white	41, 72

Soup, brown, No. 1	106
" " No. 2	106
" cream of celery	80
" cream of potato	79
" cream of tomato	80
" stock	36
" vegetable	64
Spinach, to boil	107
Steak, Salisbury	31
" to broil a	30
Stock, celery	78
" mixed	106
Stuffing for fish	101
" for pork	75
" for poultry	74
Tapioca, creamed	95
Tea, beef	39
Tea, green, to make	41
" oolong, to make	41
Toast	31
" creamed	72
" dipped	72
" French	116
" tropical	116
Tomatoes, baked	102
" to prepare	99
Turnips, to boil	37
Veal chops, to sauté	43
" pot pie	79
" to stew	38
Wafers, ginger	91
Yeast, compressed	49
" liquid	55

www.ingramcontent.com/pod-product-compliance
Lightning Source LLC
Chambersburg PA
CBHW020103170426
43199CB00009B/373